Bringing The Word From Africa

Cradle of Civilization Birthplace of Christianity

Roger Phillips Sr., PhD

McClure Publishing, Inc.

McClure™
Publishing

ISBN 13: 978-0-9915335-0-3

LCCN: 2014936323

Cover Design Image by David Dickerson
Interior Layout by Kathy McClure
Front Cover Photo Credit: Lowell Riley

http://www.mcclurepublishing.com

To order additional copies, please contact:
drrphil.2012@gmail.com
or
mcclurepublishing@msn.com
800-659-4908

DEDICATION

This body of work is dedicated to my beloved mother *Maryette Phillips-Garrett*, who is reading and bearing witness to its authenticity in Heaven. She was most influential in my life and I thank God for allowing her to be in my life 66 years as mother, matriarch and advisor.

I especially dedicate this work to my true love soul mate, partner, advisor, friend, prayer warrior and wife *Virgie*. Thank You for being there, believing and encouraging me every day. This project would not have been possible without your support and daily reminder of, *"Don't get ahead of God."* The Bible says *"Whoso findeth a wife findeth a good thing, and obtaineth favour of the Lord." (Proverbs 18:22 KJV)*

This text teaches us that God's favor is upon all men who carry out His original creative purpose. The fruit of this immense project confirms and attest to that fact, *Bless God for favor and for Lady Virgie Davie- Phillips*.

To my *amazing* children *Roger Jr., Christian Jon, Raven,* and *Morgen* and my most precious seeds, the grand babies; *Roger III, Christina, Jeremiah* Pharaoh and *Christian Jon Jr*. You are the pillars of my life and I Love You immeasurably.

Less of Me Father, More of You....

    Dr Roger Phillips Sr

ACKNOWLEDGMENT

I would like to acknowledge the many people in my life who have been an inspiration and sources of strength through this process for more than six years. To all my personal friends, colleagues, fellow expositors and prognosticators of this glorious gospel, I salute you for your patience with me and your unconditional love. I think back to my mentor and teacher, Apostle Jeffery Robinson, and all of the long tedious hours of impartations under his tutelage, and I still hear his words; *"Always see beyond what you see."* Thank You sir! so very much. To my late night telephone prayer partner and dear friend Pastor Michael Johnson, PhD, thanks for praying with and for me as I was writing and researching this powerful work. It was because of your wisdom and insight that I always dug deeper to show myself approved of God.

Special thanks to all of my family Joyce, Arlette, Deborah, Patricia and Paul. As my sisters and brother you have no idea how remarkable your presence in my life has been. Latonya, Erica, Lee, Lesley, James, Justin, Charles, Peter, Kevin, Covita, the Twins. God bless my extended family, Daphine, Michael, Bianca, Myah, Bailey, Jeanne, Bernard, Delphine, Latoya and Dr Michelle Robinson. Special thanks for the opportunity you have graced me with, Bishop Jacqueline Gordon, Shiloh New Christian Center

Melbourne, Florida. Also, Bishop Derrick Triplett, Bishop Cedric James, Bishop Tyrone Harrington, Overseer Ronnie Lee, Overseer Yvonne Jones, Bishop Charles Hawkins, Dr Ramona Joseph, the Elders, Ministers, Deacons of my local fellowship assembly who have allowed me to serve alongside of you.

To my church family, I humbly give you my gratitude for allowing me to be for some of you, a spiritual guide, teacher and friend. To the many students and *"new Christians"* whom I have had an opportunity to instruct in new members classes, thank you for hearing me and allowing me to give you valuable information concerning the Gospel and kingdom building. Finally, my most genuine and sincere admiration to many who have in some way contributed to my life in helping me in my Christian walk, no matter how diminutive or few words of encouragement, I speak God's blessings upon your life.

My prayer is that God will continue to grace me with a discerning heart in order that I might lead well and craft correct decisions. *"We should not ask God to do for us what He wants to do through us. Instead ask God to give us the wisdom to know what to do and the courage to follow through on it."*

Grace and Serenity

Overseer Roger Phillips Sr PhD

CONTENTS

FORWARD
PROLOGUE

CHAPTER 1:
CHRISTOS: THE BEGINNING 21

CHAPTER 2:
THE GARDEN OF EDEN 29

CHAPTER 3:
NOAH'S SONS: PROGENITORS OF THE RACES 47

CHAPTER 4:
ABRAHAM AND THE PROMISE..................................... 61

CHAPTER 5:
IDENTITY THEFT 75

CHAPTER 6:
BIRTH OF EMMANUEL 83

CHAPTER 7:
DOCTRINAL MESSAGE 95

CHAPTER 8:
INFANCY OF CHRISTIANITY 103

EPILOGUE

THE FOREWORD

Bringing the Word from Africa Cradle of Civilization the Birthplace of Christianity

The Redactor Dr. Luke as he addressed Theophilus in the Gospel of Luke making this profound salutation; "these former treatise I write unto you Church of the Living God; it seems good to me to write to you concerning those things that pertain to all that Jesus the Christ began to do and to teach" in relationship to Christos the Beginning. We understand that the 8ᵗʰ day is in Christos and Christos was the first of all that was created and made. This work has opened up to the reader the thoughts about the beginning of God's Image.

As the writer addresses the Beginning, we must ask the question which all of humanity has asked at one time or another, and that is where did humanity begin, who was in the beginning and how did it begin? There have been many stories, myths, fables, fallacies, ideologies, and philosophies concerning the beginning and the scholarship to its truth. As you read this work, the author will suggest an encyclopedic wealth of knowledge.

The author of this work has addressed his thorough examination of The Cradle of Civilization and the progenitor-ship of the Word of Yeshua. Through much clinical research and discovery this work pinpoints the location which we now call the continent of Africa the birthplace of all humanity, God's people and Christianity the first Faith. This valuable research fostering dedication and expounding on the intrinsic and extrinsic mapping of the historical and geographical Truths, will re-conceptualize the scholarship and theology of mankind throughout the continents.

What a wonderful and mind challenging work which will impact the seminary world and religious praxis from Alexandria to Oxford University; the libraries in Princeton and the College of Bishops, will cry out for copies to teach their Ecclesia. After reading this work they will as the author did begin to investigate the academic malpractice and the spiritual mis-education which has been historically taught by scholars and theologians in the millennium.

This work is a testimony to the great praxis in the field of apologetics concerning the intrinsic value and the extrinsic strength of Afro-centric presence historically hidden throughout the ages. As we look into the birth of a new world order where dominating geo-political leaders has already begun to map out a one world religion, and one world church, we must begin to understand the same geo-political leaders will further change and systematically delete the TRUTH of the inception of Mankind. So, in light of that theology, the author has given to us the Apostolic beginning in Christos which must be systematically delivered to the world expeditiously.

Dr. Roger Phillips Sr. PhD., A Chicagoan has brought forth a massaging wealth of encyclopedic information and knowledge which will exercise and stimulate the intrinsic thoughts and reflections that will build the present contemporary praxis and question the endless theological past, illuminating the consciousness of all that believe in Jehovah God. Time is of the essence and delivery of this Truth of Humanities beginning in God's Cradle must be magnified, vocalized, and harmonized because of its silence and encapsulation. Though Babel was willed to a place of miscommunication by being scattered, we are now able to speak as free men in the wisdom of God.

I have had the unique opportunity to view and, the pleasure of observing this work from its inception. This brilliant vessel that God has so predestined to complete this work honors me and has done me proud as his mentor and teacher by exercising the teachings of the Sons of Gideon. As God has Kenosiszed and challenged the theology of the endless past dispensational through Dr. Phillips, the theologians and scholars of the future have much to investigate as their minds are stretched, enlightened, and broadly illuminated by this work.

Dr. Roger Phillips Sr. earned his PhD in the Philosophy discipline of Biblical/Theological Studies in 2013. He also earned his Masters and Bachelor degrees in Biblical Studies from Newburgh Theological Seminary and Bible College with honors maintaining a cumulative GPA of 3.80. Dr Phillips has presently been accepted into his 2nd PhD program which focuses in Sacred Divinity. As a member of the Sons of Gideon, an elite team of expositors purposed to train and re-train the Ecclesia. Dr. Phillips has earned unquestionable credentials as a Minister, Senior Elder, and Overseer-Vicar to the office of the Presiding Prelate of New Century Fellowship of Churches and Ministries International.

He also sits on the Board of Regents at a prominent Bible college and Seminary in the southeast. He sits as Professor of Biblical studies at Chicago Baptist Institute International, Vice-Chair and teaching instructor at the Sons of Gideon Learning Institute and is currently newly appointed Dean, and Dean of Ecclesiastical Training of Christian Education in Melbourne Florida at Shiloh New Christian Center.

Apostle Jeffrey L. Robinson

PROLOGUE

This body of work will discuss in-depth the many processes of God's Word delivered into the earth realm. It will discuss various ways in which this may have been accomplished, as well as the methods stemming from the creation of humanity in the Garden of Eden and its precise location, then and now. We will examine the far reaching relationships that those times promoted and what it all means to humanity today. As we journey through the actual lands in graphic detail, we will examine and analyze detailed maps and documents describing land masses which have shifted and disappeared after catastrophic events. The end goal and purpose is to view and investigate existing land masses and those which are no longer in existence. We will confront the hidden or unspoken issues surrounding the location of the Garden of Eden thus, the cradle of civilization as well as unmitigated truths concerning the birthplace of Christianity. From the fall of man we will examine; the seeds of Adam, remnants from Noah's flood, progenitors of the races from Noah's sons, Abraham, the father of the faith and nations, genealogy of Jesus and the effects of His gifting the world with Grace Dispensation, Salvation, A New Covenant and the Apostolic Doctrinal message. Our narrative will bring to life the human footprints made and their challenges throughout history to deliver this Word, this "glorious gospel," which is the world's best-selling literary work known to man.

Our goal is not to argue but to augment the message of Yeshua, and how things would be so much better in the world by placing a strong desire and emphasis on obedience. This small attribute has impacted the world throughout the ages. We will exegetically put forth the message of Christ and bring to life why the teachings of Jesus loom so important and how it impacts Christians' lives in this dispensation of time. Our goal in this body of work is to bring clarity and focus on the beginning of the Message regarding the people who are responsible in large measure yet forgotten, and personalities which go a long way in shaping attitudes of humanity or believers as well as non-believers. Our intentions are to demonstrate how and where the message of Christ originated, the historical era dispositions and attitudes which prevail even in modern times. Our research will reveal how many other doctrinal messages have contributed to humanity either in a positive or negative manner. We will explore the question whether these doctrinal messages are that of Christ, or merely man's thoughts which he has conceived within the confines of his own mind. Who occupies that small strip of land today, as well as; are these occupiers (Jewish people who live in Israel) true heirs of the "Promise Land," according to God's Word? Who is really God's "chosen people?" Our hope is that after reading this work one may be convicted and reach greater understanding of the attitudes and the thought processes of the people of that era, gleaning for your discernment a broader yet clearer picture of how we think the masses should advance the doctrine of the "original message." It is our desire that upon reading this narrative one can remain open-minded and be receptive to revelatory truths which are rarely spoken of in the institutions and churches throughout our nation and the world. The Bible teaches us that, "…there is nothing new under the sun…" (Ecclesiastes 1:9) (KJV) Our goal at-large is not to try and re-invent the proverbial wheel. Nevertheless, we do want to highlight the squeaks of untruths when we hear them and place the oil of His anointing power of truth and wisdom on the wheel of understanding. The method we will employ to convey these thoughts will be Exegesis. This is a critical explanation or interpretation of a text, especially a religious text. Our primary focus used for exegesis of the Bible in contemporary usage will be to broaden its meaning for the reader in an extremely critical explanation of text, and the term "Biblical exegesis," will be executed here for greater specificity. The goal of Biblical exegesis is to explore the meaning of the text which then leads to discovering its significance or relevance. More specific, our style will be to lean upon Biblical Exegesis, rather than to our own understanding or engage in the process of forwarding man's personal theology, for it means absolutely nothing in the greater sense. Exegesis, as used in this body of work will include focusing primarily on the written text and a wide range of critical disciplines, textual criticism and investigation into the history and origins of the specific text. Our exegesis methodology will include the study of the historical and cultural backgrounds of the author of the text and the original audience for further in-depth clarity. Other analysis will include classification of the type of literary genres present in the text and an analysis of grammatical and syntactical features in and of the text itself. Only God's Word and doctrinal message matters and we will attempt to deliver this with stupendous clarity like never before concerning subjects which have too long been silenced or plainly ignored. In conclusion, it is our aim to substantiate the fact that "Bringing the Word from Africa," is indeed the clarion call and partnered with Africa being the "Cradle of Civilization." Our final analysis in this body of work will also show quite succinctly that the continent of Africa was indeed the "Birthplace of Christianity, "and the actual birthplace of "The Messiah," Jesus Christ with the sole purpose of restoring God's people back into a right relationship with Him and gaining the gift of salvation that all humanity would dwell in His presence and gain eternal life.

Chapter 1

CHRISTOS: THE BEGINNING

The term "Beginning," as referred to in this narrative is a title for Christ, which describes His existence before time began. Another term used to describe His being is called, "Christos." This speaks to the deity of Christ before the "kenosis." The Gospel of John teaches us that Jesus was present with God "In the beginning," and the silence of the text promotes the notion therefore that He was the Creator of all things.[1]

> "And He is the head of the body, the church; who is the beginning, the firstborn from the dead; that in all things he might have the preeminence." (Colossians 1:18) (KJV)

Christ is called the "beginning of the creation of God and the beginning and the

---

[1] Nelson's Illustrated Bible Dictionary, Thomas Nelson Publishers, Page 142

end."[2] The Bible once again confirms this statement,

> "And unto the angel of the church of the Laodiceans write; these things saith the Amen, the faithful and the true witness, the beginning of the creation of God." (Revelation 3:14) (KJV)

The word "Amen," is conveyed in the manner to infer, truly or truth. Again, the silence of the text promotes the fact that this is the One who began creating all things in the very beginning. In addition, it could not mean that He was the first to be created by God, for He is an uncreated and eternal being. Thus, we come upon the divine method of "kenosis." This is a theological term used in connection with the dual nature of Jesus as fully human and fully divine. The word comes from a Greek verb which means "to empty."[3]

> "Who, being in the form of God, thought it not robbery to be equal with God; But made himself of no reputation, and took upon him the form of a servant, and was made in the likeness of men: and being found in fashion as a man, he humbled

---

[2] Nelson's Illustrated Bible Dictionary, Thomas Nelson Publishers, Page 142

[3] Nelson's Illustrated Bible Dictionary, Thomas Nelson Publishers, Page 613

himself and became obedient unto death, even the death of the cross."

(Philippians 2:6-8) (KJV)

In this process Christ remanded Himself from the divine form to human form and from sinless humanity to a sinful and corrupt nature, which was found in His greatest creation, man. The Apostle Paul was explaining the "form of God" by saying that Christ was subsisting in the form of God, wherein He was from eternity, and had appeared to the inhabitants of heaven. However, Christ did not feel that this equality with God should be held onto or retained after entering humanity as man. So as His infinite wisdom dictated, He beforehand emptied Himself of divinity, poured back into Himself humanity, assumed the form of a servant and very much became like man. Though he was born of a virgin woman, He was not created by man, but in and unto Himself created He Him. His was God-form or God body, the Spirit body which He lived in from eternity, until taking on human form in an earthly vessel manifested in flesh during His life on earth. Void of His glory that He had with the Father before the world, His authority in Heaven and in earth, which was given back to Him by Him, after the resurrection, gave way to His outward powers which He also had before the foundations of the world. Quite simply put, if He saw Satan fall from Heaven, then it would speak to the fact that He was "in the beginning."

> "And He said unto them, I beheld Satan as lightning fall from Heaven." (Luke 10:18) (KJV)

This is where it becomes important to study Christology. He had no powers to do miracles, heal, deliver or set free until He received the Holy Spirit. Limited to the status of man, He could do nothing of Himself, until that moment wherein he received the power of the Holy Ghost and thereafter all His works, doctrines, powers, New Covenant and Great Commission instructions came under His anointing and thus His work was complete and He returned to Heaven and "sitteth at the right-hand of God." Satan was cast from Heaven long before Adam and since then, has regained dominion of the earth by Adam's fall.

As we view Christos, it becomes clearer how He made Himself like unto men and their sinful nature. Yet, He was without sin. He had to no doubt adopt the flesh which was sinful from the time of Adam in order that humanity could be redeemed and purchased back for God's intended purpose. God will not "tabernacle" in and amongst unclean vessels.

Therefore, He had to void Himself of His "very nature," His "Nephesh."The operative word in the Hebrew means, "Pure essence." Later in our narrative we will see how the many doctrinal messages of man have strayed from the original message of Christ which has served to drive a wedge between God and His people. We have already discussed God's purpose for sending forth a "Savior" into the earth in order to reconcile men's hearts and minds back unto Himself, the way it was in the Garden before the enemy came to "steal, kill and destroy." After the teachings, the passion and sacrifice of Christ; those who would adhere to this message of "death, burial, resurrection," and disciple others instructing them on how to come nigh His dwelling, were called Christians; hearers, followers and teachers of the Word. Therein, I raise the questions who are those who expound a different philosophical view and speak over the people in untruths and misnomers contrary to the Word? Who are they that place themselves at the helm of non-belief? For if one walks in unbelief it easily stands to reason they are steeped in false faith. Who are those who shepherd the people for their own "gratification?" Who are those who seek after financial gain rather than the hearts of men to be free? Who are those behind the institutions which have enormous power and influence who readily pervert the Word of God all in the proposed name of Christianity? What form and whose' form of Christianity is promulgated here? Christ came and wrapped Himself in the filth of humanity, He came that all men might receive the gift of salvation through His sufferings, He came that men might know that He was the Lamb of God, the "ram in the bush", "a way of escape," shedding His blood covering humanity giving them a comfort level of His resting peace. Why have some, in the name of Christianity contrived and perverted this message with "man conceived" doctrinal beliefs perpetrated upon the nations and in many cases, do the opposite of the Word of God. If the Incarnation as a concrete event in space and time is rejected by some, then in reality; so is the Bible rejected as well. Unless God was present in Palestine first through his powerful acts for His people of Israel and then in the life, death, resurrection; then the whole of Christianity is false and its historical truths are not taken seriously. If taken seriously and man possessed a real fear of God, vital statistics and normality's would not have been changed or tampered with or purposed to convey false doctrine.

Let's be clear, the Gospel was conceived, born, taught, exampled, recorded and "sent forth" from the continent of Africa. It was matured there, it shed blood there, it birthed it's most prominent leaders and patriarchs in this very land which was the cradle of civilization. It was this land that God chose to come and "tabernacle" amongst His people. It was this land that He chose to sacrifice His life. And, it was this land that He chose to "begin life for all humanity." We believe that it is important that the prevailing conversation regarding Christianity, Christology and the "original message" doctrine be placed upon the record once and for all with the type of clarity and facts this dissertation will undertake. Shaleak Ben Yehuda, keeper of the Temple of the Seal of Wisdom in Jerusalem offers these thoughts, "History must desperately backtrack in giant steps to acknowledge facts before it can begin to attempt to fulfill its prophetic destiny in a reconciliatory acknowledgement of truth (salvation) or else it will plunge onward to sure destruction, doom and disaster never before known to the inhabitants of the earth." The presence of African influence is very prevalent in the shaping of Christianity and the telling of the Word to all the nations. That presence and reestablishment of these facts must carry the day and our European brothers must retreat to the rear and wait to receive the Gospel as it was accorded. They are not the progenitors of Christianity. They are but an extension of its important message and somewhere along the way upon them receiving this message hundreds of years later, they have re-formed, reshaped, and created images of its main source characters to fit local cultures and delegated authority grossly misplaced. The likelihood of this glorious gospel originating from another continent other than this land mass now called Africa, is at best nil and the record will support this after all the facts are examined in this volume of work. Our narrative will reveal and uncover many factual truths and information which will be telling but controversial, for these truths must prevail and "his-story" must be given a full and accurate descriptive account.

Chapter 2

THE GARDEN OF EDEN

The Garden of Eden, as is told was the beginning of humanity and the creation of earth, animals and all living and breathing things, the firmament, dividing of the waters under and above, the light of the sun, moon and stars. First, let's establish the area which is spoken of in the Bible. We will reference the Bible(s) in great measure in this narrative as it is the most published book in the world and it is a historical record of the relationship between a particular people and Jehovah-Elohim, the eternal Creator.

> "These are the generations of the heavens and of the earth when they were created, in the day that the Lord God made the earth and the heavens." (Genesis 2:4) (KJV)

It is the specialness of that relationship which has affected the entire world. The origin of the people of that time has mystified many and according to whose account you choose to believe, determines ones end belief. One issue could very well be the misinterpretations of those who rendered the original translations from Hebrew and Greek into Latin, English and other languages. It can be proposed and advanced that a large portion of the confusion stems perhaps from deliberate "Eurocentric" and centuries of "Euro-Americans" attempts to conceal, what today would be called the racial and or ethnic identity of the people of the Bible. The Book of Genesis outlines the beginning. The Hebrew word for Genesis is, "bereshit," the beginning. In this time-frame known as the Antediluvian Age or the story of "re-creation," chaos is ended and order restored and all things are brought back into existence by God's Word or a second habitable state.

Light is restored and the "Spirit of God hovers over the waters." The unfrozen waters, warmed by the sun "gives life," with animals which are,

> "...made after his kind, and cattle after their kind and everything that creepeth upon the earth after his kind:" (Genesis 1:25) (KJV)

Made, or the Hebrew word "asah," means to make out of already existing material, being the opposite of "bara," which means to create. In Genesis 1:21, God rearranged and restored matter. He in turn introduced life which did not require constructive, but creative powers.

> "...and God made two great lights...He made the stars also..." (Genesis 1:16) (KJV)

God created man,

> "...great whales, and every living creature that moveth, which the waters brought forth...." (Genesis 1:21) (KJV)

To create, means to bring something into being that was not there before, to create anew.

The geographical characteristics of this area can be summarized by the uniformity of climatic conditions, the diversity of its land forms as well as the contrast of its two major hydrographic systems, The Nile River and The Tigris-Euphrates. Even now throughout the Near East regions, the climate is an extreme variety of the Mediterranean regime. The winters are mild to fairly cold, depending on altitude. Summers are hot to extreme according to altitudinal differences. For example, heat temperatures can reach 113-118 degrees in the Jordan Valley, compared with 95-100 degrees on the coastal plains of Palestine. There are persistent westerly winds due to the low barometric pressure which prevail for successive weeks and months during summer. With the disappearance of this pressure pattern in winter, depressions from the Mediterranean reach into the Near East, providing a variability of wind direction familiar to King Solomon, writer of Ecclesiastes.

"The wind goeth toward the south and turneth about unto the north, it whirleth about continually, and the wind returneth again according to his circuits." (Ecclesiastes 1:6) (KJV)

God created humanity after satan fell from heaven due to his rebellious behavior. After his fall the earth was thrown into what was known as the Anti-Chaotic Age. In brief, this period was divided into nine dispensations. This will be discussed later, but in order to fill a void of praisers and worshippers to His majesty and glory, God created humanity to take the place of satan in praising Him. The Garden of Eden was where this creation took place and as we've described the prevailing climate in this region, we will begin the narrative on its exact location, relative to the land masses of that time period.

At or even before the Mesozoic Era, Africa was joined with earth's other continents in Pangaea. The Mesozoic Era was an interval of geological time from about 250 million years ago to about 65 million years ago. It is often referred to as the age of reptiles because reptiles, namely dinosaurs; were the dominant terrestrial and marine vertebrates of that time. This was a time of climatic and evolutionary activity. The name Pangaea, which means "all land," refers to a supercontinent which existed during this period forming 300 million years ago and began to break-up approximately 200 million years ago. During a symposium in 1927 Alfred Wegener's theory of continental drift was discussed at length describing the supercontinent called "urkontinent", before its breaking up and drifting to their current locations. Fossil evidence for Pangaea includes the presence of similar and identical species on continents that are now great distances apart. Additional evidence is found for Pangaea in the geology of adjacent continents, including matching geological trends between the eastern coasts of South America and the western coast of Africa.[4] (Illustration Map No. 1)

The Anti-chaotic Age comes into play as it is better known as the dateless past, from the end of the 7 days of Genesis 1:3 and Genesis 2:25. This time frame is also known as the Dispensation of Angels, because angels ruled various planets.

[4] Wikipedia.org/wiki/Pangaea, Wikipedia The Free Encyclopedia

"Thou has been in Eden, the garden of God; every precious stone was thy covering, the sardius, topaz and the diamond, the beryl, the onyx and the jasper, the sapphire, the emerald, and the carbuncle, and gold; the workmanship of thy tabrets and of thy pipes was prepared in thee in the day that thou wast created. Thou art the anointed cherub that covereth, and I have set thee so; thou was upon the holy mountain of God; thou hast walked up and down in the midst of the stones of fire. Thou wast perfect in thy ways from the day that thou wast created, till iniquity was found in thee. By the multitude of thy merchandise they have filled the midst of thee with violence, and thou hast sinned; therefore, I will cast thee as profane out of the mountain of God, and I will destroy thee, O covering cherub, from the midst of the stones of fire. Thine heart was lifted up because of thy beauty; thou hast corrupted thy wisdom by reason of thy brightness; I will cast thee to the ground, I will lay thee before kings, that they may behold thee. Thou hast defiled thy sanctuaries by the multitude of thine iniquities, by the iniquity of thy traffic; therefore will I bring forth a fire from the midst of thee; it shall devour thee, and I will bring thee to ashes upon the earth in the sight of all them that behold thee." (Ezekiel 28:13-18) (KJV)

The world that then was, is now flooded by God's wrath of judgment.

> "And saying, where is the promise of His coming? For since the fathers fell asleep, all things continue as they were from the beginning of the creation. For this they are willingly ignorant of, that by the word of God the heavens were of old, and the earth standing out of the water and in the water: Whereby the world that then was, being overflowed with water, perished." (2 Peter 3:4-6) (KJV)

This is the kosmos or social system which embraced the entire pre-Adamite universe that all fossils belong. After flooding, God withheld the light of the sun, moon and stars and darkness fell upon the earth and it froze over into the "ice age."

> "I beheld the earth, and lo, it was without form, and void; and the heavens, and they had no light. I beheld the mountains, and lo, they trembled, and all the hills moved lightly. I beheld, and, lo, there was no man, and all the birds of the heavens were fled. I beheld and, lo, the fruitful place was a wilderness, and all the cities were broken down at the presence of the Lord, and by his fierce anger. For thus hath the Lord said, the whole land shall be desolate, yet 1 will not make a full end. For this shall the

earth mourn, and the heavens above be black, because I have spoken it, I have purposed it, and I will not repent, neither will I turn back from it. (Jeremiah 4:23-28) (KJV)

Man was created and placed in the Garden of Eden, somewhere purposed in southwest Asia, the approximate geographic center of the largest land portion of the earth's surface at that time. (Ancient map Illustration (Map Illustration No. 2))[5] This is known today as Africa and the Middle East, depending upon which area of the land mass one accepts as the ancient place of the garden. Our research has found two possible locations based upon the scriptures as it describes the various rivers running out of the garden and/or encompassing the garden.

"And a river went out of Eden to water the garden; and from thence it was parted, and became four heads. The name of the first is Pison: that is it which compasseth the whole land of Havilah, where there is gold; And the gold of that land is good: there is bdellium and the onyx stone. And the name of the second river is Gihon; the same is it that compasseth the whole land

---

[5] Halley's Bible Handbook, Zondervan Publishing House, Page 24

of [Ethiopia]. And the name of the third river is Hiddekel; that is it which goeth toward the east of Assyria. And the fourth river is Euphrates." (Genesis 2:10-14) (KJV).

We find the second location of the garden or the creation of the first human (Homo sapiens) took place in the heart of Biblical Africa. The rivers spoken of in the scripture verify human existence in this area. Archaeologists and scientists confirm without doubt the oldest form of human life has been discovered around the Olduvai Gorge in present day Tanzania which dates back some 200,000 years ago.[6] The map illustration depicts how humankind found their way to other parts of the known world. By illustration, this move was toward northeast Africa, the "Middle East," and from there into Asia and Europe. (Map Illustration No. 3) It suggests that during the Biblical days when civilization was high in Kemet (Egypt) there was little known activity on the continent we know today as Europe. It further states that civilization came late to the Caucasians of the north and that which came, was brought forth from Akebu-lan (Africa), which is referred to here as the "Mother of all Lands." (Ancient

---

[6] Original African Heritage Edition Holy Bible, James C. Winston Publishing Company, Nashville, Tennessee, Page 107

Map Illustration (Map Illustration No. 4))[7] We can clearly establish with common sense the ancestral home of humanity was in the land of Africa. Before the land mass was separated it was all one land mass. The name Africa is actually of Latin origin and was imposed on this continent by European explorers. In Biblical studies one will never find the names of England or Germany mentioned in any scripture. The Old Testament on the other hand mentions Ethiopia over forty times and Egypt over one-hundred times.

After Lucifer's fall, all the earth was flooded in God's judgment and the light from the sun; moon and stars were withheld causing the earth to be cold, dark and desolate.

> "By what way is the light parted, which scattereth the east wind upon the earth? Who hath divided a watercourse for the overflowing of waters, or a way for the lightning of thunder," (Job 38:24-25) (KJV).

> "Out of whose womb came the ice? And the hoary frost of heaven, who hath gendered it? The waters are hid as with a

---

[7] Original African Heritage Edition Holy Bible, James C. Winston Publishing Company, Nashville Tennessee, Page 107 Map 5

stone, and the face of the deep is frozen."
(Job 38:29-30) (KJV).

Now comes the restoration of earth after
thousands of years in this existing state. God,
by His Word spoke all things back into
existence as a place for humanity to inhabit and
maintain an obedient relationship with Him. He
gave man the ability to name all the animals and
all living things in the earth. He also gave him
dominion over all things, yet he had to remain
obedient and not partake in eating from the
"tree in the midst of the garden." It did not
matter why man could not eat from the tree;
God said it and that should have settled it.

As we have noted with the map illustrations,
this beautiful "garden of life," was located
geographically covering thousands of square
miles from the now continent of Asia, to as far
south as the land of Ethiopia where the River
Nile runs through. Again, depending on which
location one accepts, the Bible says that "a river
went out of Eden," and, "was parted, and
became into four heads." There are some who
believe that because the Bible speaks of the
"tree of life by the river," the location is in
Judah somehow or another that would more
than likely have been the place of the original
Garden of Eden. This could very well be,
however; the garden would have been a vast

place of "source of life," and to pinpoint or relegate this area to too within a rather small patch of land would only serve to limit God's creative abilities and untold powers. In other words, I find it difficult to see how an historian of any significance or stature could propose and advance the notion that the garden was a small patch of land located in Jerusalem or "Salem" back then. Of course, we are not pointing the finger at any one individual, but merely stating that the awesome power of God should not nor cannot, be limited in any way. "The name of the second river is Gihon: the same is it that compasseth the whole land of Ethiopia." The textual meaning of the word "compasseth," in the Hebrew means, "to revolve, surround or border; bring, cast, fetch, lead, make, walk, whirl, roundabout, be about on every side...."[8] One can clearly see where Ethiopia is located on various maps during that time period as well as now. The text states also that, "The name of the first river is Pison: that is it which compasseth the whole land of Havilah." The land once known as Havilah is today Saudi Arabia, and the distance from the two rivers (compasseth both lands) is approximately

---

[8] The New Strong's Exhaustive Concordance of the Bible, Hebrew and Aramaic Dictionary, Page 97 Main Concordance Page 217, Thomas Nelson Publishers, Nashville

1,886.43 kilometers or 1,172.17 miles apart.[9] The Greeks called the land Cush, where the first two rivers named flowed. This term would later be transposed as "Aithiops," or Ethiopia, meaning literally "burnt face people." The scripture connects the Pishon River with Havilah, a direct descendant of Cush as depicted in Genesis 10:7. The Gihon River as cited in the text is the second river in Eden surrounding the whole land of Cush/Ethiopia. This is indeed a clear indication that wherever Eden extended, its beginning was within the continent of Africa. As our map illustration purposes, humankind migrated throughout the world from the land of Ethiopia located on the continent of Africa. Old Testament scripture was written based upon events and characters developed from African/Edenic roots which is then traced to the land of Canaan, which was but an extension of the African peoples who frequently migrated from the continent proper through Canaan/Palestine to the east toward what was then included as Asia or the "Fertile Crescent" or the Tigris and Euphrates rivers of ancient Mesopotamia. Up until 1869 and the building of the Suez Canal the Middle East was connected with the continent of Africa and the

---

[9] Truth Knowledge, the Internet Answer Engine, wwwtruthknowledge.com/q/facts_about_mile

man-made separation has affected not only the land but its cultural and social fabrics. It was during World War II when correspondents introduced the name Middle East, for the portion of land separated from the main portion of the African continent. Prior to that time this area was known as northeast Africa. Various openings of scriptures speak of Egypt and Ethiopia which both at one time was considered one in the same and very often in the Bible they are synonymous. (Map Illustration No. 5) The term Egypt was once used to mean all of Africa which was called the "Land of Ham."

> "Israel also came into Egypt; and Jacob sojourned in the land of Ham. And he increased his people greatly, and made them stronger than their enemies. He turned their heart to hate his people, to deal subtly with his servants. He sent Moses, his servant, and Aaron, whom he had chosen. They showed his signs among them, and wonders in the land of Ham." (Psalm 105:23-27) (KJV)

> "And smote all the firstborn in Egypt, the chief of their strength in the tabernacles of Ham." (Psalm 78:51) (KJV)

> "They forgat God, their Saviour, which had done great things in Egypt, Wondrous works in the land of Ham, and terrible things by the Red sea." (Psalm106:21-22) (KJV)

In conclusion, regarding the original location of the Garden of Eden, we are shown without a doubt its location was on the continent of Africa. The remaining rivers mentioned in scripture, that of the Tigris and Euphrates Rivers is today in Iraq. This is a land rich in places related to events of Biblical history, Ur of the Chaldees where Abraham was born about 2000 B.C., Nineveh, the capital of The Assyrian Empire that conquered the northern tribes of Israel in 721 B.C., and Babylon the ancient capital of the Babylonian Empire which conquered the southern kingdom of Judah in 586 B.C. There have been many modern day searches for the original garden but to relatively no avail. This would be probable given the fact of Noah's flood changing the landscape and obliterating the entire region so that no one would be able to find its source of life. God wanted it this way after all, He placed judgment upon humanity and Satan; He ousted them all from the garden never to return in man's present state of being ... that of flesh. "Therefore the Lord God sent him forth from the garden of Eden..."

"So He drove out the man; and He placed at the east of the garden of Eden Cherubims, and a flaming sword which turned every way, to keep the way of the tree of life." (Genesis 3:23-24) (KJV)

We as humanity can never return to the garden in the form of this earthly vessel we possess, our return can only be in the form and in the way in which God created man... in His likeness. This likeness of course is Spirit. Though closely secluded from the rest of the world, Africa still no doubt lies at the gateway of all the loftiest and noblest traditions of the human race. Africa and the Garden of Eden are synonymous to one another as they intermingle with all the Divine administrations and as revealed in this narrative, well connected in one way or another with some of the most famous names and events in the annuals of time. Abram, the progenitor of the Hebrew race and the founder of their religion sought refuge in Africa. Jacob and his sons were saved in the same way by seeking refuge in the land. God's loyal servant Moses, was born and educated in Africa; finally hundreds of years later, the Incarnated Son of God; during infancy, was preserved from death in the great land of Egypt after being born, not in the Middle East, but in the land of Africa where as Christos (the Beginning) formed the Garden of Eden in the conscience of His mind, to place His greatest creation here, even before the foundations of the world. It would stand to reason that if the region from which the biblical Garden of Eden extends was known then as northeast Africa, then map makers and lay-truth seekers alike, should have no problem accepting Africa as the cradle of civilization. Eden, this land of pleasure and delight was a place of special joy to God. In this beautiful "garden of life," where God placed humanity, in order for us to find our way "back to Eden and sit on top of the world," we must rediscover the image and likeness in which God created us in the first place.

Chapter 3

NOAH'S SONS, PROGENITORS OF THE RACES

Ham was one of Noah's three sons and progenitor of the African people.

> "For if God spared not the angels that sinned, but cast them down to hell, and delivered them into chains of darkness, to be reserved unto judgment; And spared not the old world, but saved Noah, the eighth person, a preacher of righteousness, bringing in the flood upon the world of the ungodly..." (2 Peter 2:4-5) (KJV)

Noah, his wife and sons: Shem, Ham, Japheth and their three wives were the eight people God "saved;"

> "...and Noah only remained alive, and they that were with him in the ark. And the

waters prevailed upon the earth an hundred and fifty days." (Genesis 7:23b-24) (KJV)

After the flood waters had receded Noah, his wife and three sons and their wives were sent forth to replenish the earth. It was during this time that the African patriarch Noah instituted human government. His sons went forth to establish the nations of people and the son we place our focus upon will be Ham. His sons were Cush, Mizraim, Put and Canaan. Ham is connected with the native name of Egypt, Kem, or, in full pa ta' en Kem, "the land of Egypt," in Bashmurian Coptic Kheme, is unlikely, as this form is probably of a much later date than the composition of Gen and moreover, as the Arabic shows, the guttural is not a true kh, but the hard breathing h, which are both represented by the Hebrew cheth. On the list, as being the darkest-skinned people, is Cush or Ethiopia, after which comes Mitsrayim, or Egypt, then Put or Libya, and Canaan last. The sons or descendants of each of these are then taken in turn, and it is noteworthy to mention that some of them, like the Ethiopians and the Canaanites, spoke Semitic, and not Hamitic, languages or Seba dialect if connected with the Sabeans, Havilah, Yemen/Saudi Arabia, and Sheba, whose queen Makeda visited Solomon and birthed a child from their tryst and she named him Menelik. The original home of the

Phoenicians, who spoke a Semitic language was probably based upon other tongues that were forced upon these nationalities in consequence of their migrations, or because they came under the dominion of nationalities alien to themselves. The non-Sem Babylonians, described as descendants of Nimrod, spoke Sumerian, and adopted Semitic Babylonian only as a result of intermingling with the Semites whom they found there. As we review the line of Ham, we find that sons Mizraim spun Egypt; Cush, Sudan and Ethiopia; Put, Libya and Canaan, Hivites, Jebusites, Arvadites, Girgashites, Amorites, Arkites, Sinites, Hittites, Sidonians, Perizzites, Zemarites. These cities, the earliest that are mentioned in the Bible, were uncovered by archaeologists over a century ago and have been positively identified. So also are the ancient Canaanite and Egyptian civilizations are known. Thus the setting for the Genesis narrative, the call of Abraham and his journey of faith has a historical basis to it that cannot be denied.

Let's begin to make some scriptural connections here with the descendants of Ham. Jesus spoke to the Pharisees in Matthew 12:41-42 concerning ancestral land of Ninevah and of Queen Makeda and one of Ham's nephews, Nimrod. Ninevah was the last capital of the Empire of Assyria. Nimrod is associated with this northern Mesopotamian region and is described as being one of the "evil and adulterous generation," by Jesus in Matthew 12:39. (KJV)

> "The men of Nineveh shall rise in judgment with this generation, and shall condemn it…" (Matthew 12:41) (KJV)

> "The queen of the south shall rise up in the judgment with this generation and shall condemn it; for she came from the uttermost parts of the earth to hear the wisdom of Solomon; and, behold, a greater than Solomon is here." (Matthew 12:42) (KJV)

Her long and strenuous journey to Palestine in search of righteousness was a symbol of great faith, and so Jesus, over a thousand years later in addressing the Pharisee's who were asking him for a sign proving that He was the son of God, spoke of her to the generation that existed during His time. It was a generation which refused to believe in God unless a sign was shown them. Jesus was therefore angered by their sheer unbelief, which prompted Him to address them as we have read in Matthew 12:39. As we beam our light upon Ham with greater intensity we are to understand that he was cursed by his father Noah as he shamed himself by gazing upon his father's nakedness.

"And Ham the father of Canaan, saw the nakedness of his father, and told his two brethren without." (Genesis 9:22) (KJV)

We have come to believe that Ham was cursed and therefore so were all black people of his African/Edenic heritage.

"And he said, Cursed be Canaan; a servant of servants shall he be unto his brethren." (Genesis 9:25) (KJV)

However, we ascertain through careful study of the scriptures as revealed to us by exegetical examination, that the curse was placed upon Canaan, the son of Ham. In our discovery of this Biblical knowledge, we know that Mizraim, Put and Cush were not included in this rebuke. Abraham's inheritance of the land of Canaan as his blessing was due to this prophetic pronouncement by Noah. His son Shem and his descendants received the blessing of Noah due to this strong desire to be in his father's image and his love for God.

"And he said, Blessed be the Lord God of Shem; and Canaan shall be his servant. God shall enlarge Japheth, and he shall dwell in the tents of Shem; and Canaan shall be his servant." (Genesis 9:26-27) (KJV)

Let us go forth in further unpacking this line of humanity as we examine the sons of Ham, their descendants and nations spawned through their bloodlines. Cush, was the Biblical land which is now known as Ethiopia or the Sudan. Mizraim, spawned the land of Egypt, Phut which is known today as Libya and Canaan which became known as Palestine and Israel. The sons collectively inhabited north and northeast Africa as the original inhabitants of these regions. Within this lineage of Ham was the son of Cush, who was the father of Nimrod. Ham's grandson Nimrod was known to be an eminent African hunter and architect. He was the first man to try to build his way to Heaven. In doing this he managed to draw and begin work on a gigantic tower that would allow him and his fellow servants to see Heaven as well as earth. The tower was built in a city called Babel, in the beginning of his empire.

> "And the beginning of his kingdom was Babel, and Erech, and Accad, and Calneh, in the land of Shinar." (Genesis 10:10) (KJV)

He is also considered to be the rightful innovator and builder of many such ancient Babylonian cities. Out of these great cities under Nimrod rule and building skills was Ninevah and Calah.

"Out of that land went forth Asshur and builded Nineveh and the city of Rehoboth and Calah." (Genesis 10:11) (KJV)

Now as for the curse which Noah called into existence against Canaan, Ham's son, the explanation that black Africans, as the "sons of Ham", were cursed, possibly "blackened" by their sins, was advanced only sporadically during the middle ages, but became increasingly common during the slave trade of the 18th and 19th centuries. The justification of slavery itself through the sins of Ham was well suited to the ideological interests of the elite within the European governments with the emergence of the slave trade; its radicalized version justified the exploitation of a ready supply of African labor. In the parts of Africa where Christianity flourished in the early days, while it was still illegal in Rome, this idea never took hold, and its interpretation of scripture was never adopted by the African Coptic Churches. A modern Amharic commentary on Genesis notes the 19th century and earlier European theory that blacks were subject to whites as a result of the "curse of Ham", but calls this a false teaching unsupported by the text of the Bible, emphatically pointing out that Noah's curse fell not upon all descendants of Ham, but only on the descendants of Canaan, and asserting that it was fulfilled when Canaan was occupied by both Semites (Israel) and Japhethites (ancient Philistines). What is further noted is the fact that Canaanites ceased to exist politically after the Third Punic War 149 BC and, their current descendants are thus of an unknown origin and could very well have been scattered among the world community. If we find this to be the accepted narrative of the ancient Canaanites and their possible whereabouts in that dispensation of time, then we must pose the following questions; who are the current occupiers of the land of modern Israel and where did they originate from? How does a Euro/American organization (The United Nations plan to partition Palestine-1947) decide that the people of Euro descendants are the originators of the land and have rightful inheritance to the land in question and, in doing so, disenfranchise those who are on the land that have been there since the days of Canaan, son of Ham? The curse of Noah's son was placed upon Canaan and not Ham according to scripture and it would seem that this is where the fact derives of who are the inheritors of the land versus who are not. In ancient times the Hebrews believed themselves to be Semites or direct descendants of Shem. Mr. William McKee Evans says in his writings, that if we are to believe that Noah and his sons were the progenitors of mankind after the Flood, one may envision as a result of scripture, enslavement of a people. According to Biblical accounts the enslavers and the enslaved were descendants of brothers. He goes on to say that the tradition shows at this point, that there is no color bias. Our opinion regarding color bias or non-color bias is nonexistent as they were all black-skinned, if no more than due to the climatic conditions which prevailed in the region. We agree with Mr. McKee when he states that the Hebrews of this millennium, B.C. did not associate slavery with any particular race.[10] Again not by color as a staple, for they all looked like each other. The Canaanites were a conquered people and thus were living out the curse placed upon them earlier by Noah as they came under subjection of the Davidic and Solomon newly created kingdom. All this was according to the curse,

> "...Cursed be Canaan; a servant of servants shall he be unto his brethren. And he said, Blessed be the Lord God of Shem; and Canaan shall be his servant." (Genesis 9:25-26) (KJV)

What we know is that Shem's descendants where definitely enslavers of the Canaanites. The shift from Ham to his son Canaan

---

[10] William McKee Evans, "From the Land of Canaan to the Land of Guinea: The Strange Odyssey of the Sons of Ham." The American Historical Review Volume 85 No. 1 Feb., 1980, pp 17-18) Published by: The University of Chicago Press

established the historic legitimacy of Israel's later conquest of the Canaanites.

The record clearly shows that the biblical account of a tale of distinctly non-African people who briefly sojourned in Egypt – which was somehow later removed from black Africa – before moving on to ancient Canaan which, despite its location also has been shown not to have had any relation to Africa (Middle East). We find it amazing how, throughout the annuals of historical writings, depictions of Christ were projected as Euro-Asian Hebrews and that they outright gave birth to a blond, blue-eyed Jesus who founded Christianity as an offshoot of thoroughly Hellenistic religions of the Greco-Roman Empire. The scriptures as translated in various Bibles, fortunately refuses to give in to these far-fetched notions of disbelief. As to the surprise of many who have sought out the truth revealed in the scriptures, comes as a contradiction surprise to those who distorted the facts and twisted and contorted the truth, that there existed a very real multiculturalism. When discovered, one need only apply cultural exegesis and Afro-centric biblical interpretations which have had a tendency to release the necessary understandings of parochial Eurocentric understandings. This can and has been liberating in the sense that it goes to the point of case-point-scripture, which is the knowledge base for which we have attempted to write within the body of this work, showing the origination of both humanity as well as Christianity. To put it plain and simple, many; if not all the characters of the Bible have been depicted as whole-heartedly European in diverse ecclesiastical circles and various pictorials and illustrations. In conclusion, the ancient land of Canaan was culturally and geographically an extension of the African land mass known then as Northeastern Africa. These descendants of Ham and Canaan frequently migrated east from the continent proper, through Canaan/Palestine toward the "fertile crescent" (Mesopotamia) of the famous Tigris and Euphrates Rivers. So what we have is the people who populated the so-called ancient Near East were essentially Afro-Asiatic peoples. The Greeks and Romans did not make an appearance in biblical narratives until many years later. When they came into focus in the narrative, they were always depicted as oppressors and exploiters, in stark contrast to the great civilizations of Africa, which again, are so often viewed as a source of comfort and strength. Scripture again supports this theoretical fact. Joseph and Mary were instructed by the angels to carry baby Jesus to Egypt and remain there until Herod was dead.

"And when they were departed, behold the angel of the Lord appeareth to Joseph in a dream, saying, Arise, and take the young child and his mother, and flee into Egypt, and be thou there until I bring thee word; for Herod will seek the young child to destroy him." (Matthews 2:13) (KJV)

"When Israel was a child, then I loved him, and called my son out of Egypt." (Hosea 11:1) (KJV)

In the Hebrew Bible, the frequency in which Jacob and his progeny literally sojourned in Egypt is recorded.

"Israel also came into Egypt, and Jacob sojourned in the land of Ham." (Psalm 105:23) (KJV)

The Bible teaches us that throughout this inspired word of God, Egypt is known as the "land of Ham," with Noah's son Ham as the progenitor of the African peoples.

"And smote all the first-born in Egypt, the chief of their strength in the tabernacles of Ham;" (Psalm 78:51) (KJV)

In a clarion roll-call of African people and the nations they represent, we find it distinctly clear that they are all found in biblical writings; Cush - Arabia or present day Sudan; Ethiopia and Yemen. We must remember that God instructed Joseph and Mary to flee with the child Jesus to Egypt. Why? It would be obvious, it would serve as a brilliant ingenious hiding place where Mary, Joseph and the child Jesus would "blend" in with the natives of the land and thus would be safe from the clutches of Herod. Secondly, the scriptures of prophecy had to be fulfilled and thirdly, what better place for the child Jesus to study and receive the knowledge and wisdom of those who were the seeds of the descendants of the chosen children of the promise. Medieval and Renaissance artists over years gradually changed the projected image and illustrations of Jesus. They were attempting to appease those in power and those who would pay them handsomely to utilize their skills using paints, oils and watercolors in an effort to uphold preconceived notions of those viewing from near as well as afar Christianity, as a European religion. It wasn't long before European Christian art, depicting biblical characters in false images (which were more favorable and familiar to persons of European descent) became the norm throughout the world. What we are attempting to show here is merely the fact that through the centuries of men, philosophies and ever-changing imagery, the notion has been cast that somehow European culture and wisdom overshadows ancient, darker and clearer African icons. Standing in many cathedrals of Europe,

North and South America, even the Vatican-inspired Basilica in Africa's very own Ivory Coast, the artistic representation of European values and cultures are shown to continue to perpetuate this great lie. Sadly enough, many Christians think of a black Jesus as an oddity or even a scandalous distortion of historical facts. These notions are dismissed out-of-hand that such portrayals of Jesus have any truths and are as such a frightful violation of ancient ethnology[11] insisting that Jesus was two-fold a Semitic and Middle Eastern prophet. The only thing left to say is Ham, his sons Cush, Mizraim, Canaan and his grandfather Noah and Uncles Shem and Japheth, cousins Phut, Javan, Lud, Seba, Havilah, Raamah, Nimrod, Arphaxad, Eber, Nahor, Terah, Abraham, Nahor, Lot, Ishmael, Issac, Jacob, Judah and many more, would likely say, shame on them for not speaking and projecting to the world in truth and knowledge!

---

[11] Etn-nol-o-gy, n. The branch of anthropology concerned with the classification and description of regional, chiefly primitive human cultures. Funk & Wagnalls Standard Desk Dictionary. Funk & Wagnalls Publishing Co., Inc. 1969 Library of Congress Catalog Card No. 66-25079

Chapter 4

ABRAHAM AND THE PROMISE

Abraham was a descendant of Shem and David and his son Solomon were descendants of Abraham. The informational point here is Abraham was the first Hebrew and the promise from God was that his descendants would inherit the land and the birthrights via his son Isaac and subsequently all of his heirs settling in the land of Canaan whereby the prophecy of Noah would be proven to be truly of God.

> "And I will make of thee a great nation, and I will bless thee and make thy name great; and thou shalt be a blessing."(Genesis 12:2) (KJV)

I find this text particularly important because the scripture uses the word "shalt" not "shall" wherein the latter means "continuous," in an ongoing manner. The promise of God to

Abraham that he would be heir of the "world" is repeated to his offspring.

> "For the promise that he should be the heir of the world was not to Abraham, or to his seed, through the law, but through the righteousness of faith." (Romans 4:13) (KJV)

The text clearly states that God gave the promise to Abraham and his seed not through the law, but rather by their faith .This speaks to the question, are those who are occupants of the land of modern day Israel, the original people and "the chosen people?" Now the last time I examined writings or heard any testimony from those occupants, they were acknowledging that they were Jews, therein admitting the Messiah has not come yet and they are still waiting his appearing. If we are to believe the Bible, and I for one do, without error, it clearly states that,

> "For unto us a child is born, unto us a son is given, and the government shall be upon his shoulder; and his name shall be called Wonderful, Counselor, The Mighty God, The Everlasting Father, The Prince of Peace." (Isaiah 9:6) (KJV)

This scripture is one of the most poetic promises of the Messiah's coming. This verse also contains a reference to one of the great incomprehensible truths in the Bible; The Incarnation, "a child is born." God would become a man; a newborn baby would be called "Mighty God, Everlasting Father." Those who accept that truth, accept by and through faith. Paul says that He took the form of a servant and came as a man.

> "Therefore God has exalted Him and given Him the name which is above every name." (Philippians 2:7) (KJV)

So if you have a nation of "lost people" claiming to be the heirs to the land but don't believe that the "King" was born, ministered to the people, walked the land healing, delivering and setting free, then, somewhere a fraud has been perpetrated and the people have been in large measure "duped". If Jews fundamentally do not believe that Christ was the Messiah, then than they would obviously be still held to and operate under the statures of the Mosaic Laws. The Bible once again speaks with clarity,

> "For if they which are of the law be heirs, faith is made void, and the promise made of none effect." (Romans 4:14)

Those who believe in the "saviour" and that He appeared and died , that all men might be saved through the gift of salvation ushering in the Dispensation of Grace and setting aside the law, it would seem according to scripture, they are or would be the heirs to the promise of Abraham.

> "Therefore it is of faith, that it might be by grace; to the end the promise might be sure to all the seed; not to that only which is of the law, but to that also which is of the faith of Abraham; who is the father of us all. (As it is written, I have made thee a father of many nations.) before him whom he believed, even God, who quickeneth the dead, and calleth those things which be not as though they were." (Romans 4:16-17) (KJV)

It deeply pains me to have to go to color bias, black-skinned nomenclatures or indulge the reader with racial narrative etc.; for we are all God's people created by Him in his likeness and image. However, it is very necessary and important to point out and illustrate in this body of work, that the aforementioned patriarchs of the Biblical history being forwarded, were all dark-skinned, Black African/Edenic dark people. To clarify, the occupiers of the land in Israel in 1948 upon becoming a state were Caucasians from Eastern Europe proper. They could not have been descendants of the people of Africa because climatic conditions would have played a significant role in the pigmentation of their skin and hair, based upon one's DNA adapting abilities to the environment. This would explain why so many European Jews are blond and blue eyed, with a slight Mongol slant to their eyes, as well as the total absence of Semitic features among many Israelis of European descent. I've engrossed myself in a great deal of research concerning where these people came from. I've never read they were from Africa proper, were dispersed unto the European continent over centuries, made a complexion and hair texture change and came back to possess the land as the chosen people. In 1948 over 700,000 Palestinians were expelled from the Jewish state or from their own lands. These events actually occurred as recorded in the history of that region. All this took place during the Arab-Israeli War immediately following the British Mandate expiring over the region and the Jewish Agency proclaiming independence and naming the country Israel. Israel was accepted as a member of the United Nations by majority vote on May 11, 1949. The ensuing years were marked by an influx of Holocaust survivors and Jews from various Arab lands many of whom faced persecution in and expulsion from their original countries. Consequently, the population of Israel rose from 800,000 to two million between 1948 and 1958. From 1948-1970 approximately 1,151,029 Jewish refugees relocated to Israel. The country's Law of Return grants all Jews and those of Jewish lineage the right to Israeli citizenship. Just a little over three-quarters 75.5% are Jews from a diversity of Jewish backgrounds. 22% are from Europe and the Americas and 10% are from Africa and Asia. Jews who fled Arab and Muslim countries and their descendants comprise 50% of the population. Jews from Eastern Europe and the former Soviet Union and their Israeli descendants form the remaining Jewish population.[12] Israeli Jews consider themselves to be approximately 55% traditional and 20% secular Jews.

When we speak of traditional Jewish beliefs we are reminded of one of the greatest philosophers of this tradition, Maimonides. He believed thoroughly in the Gaonic tradition, especially in its North African version, which formed the basis of his legal thought. Ironically, Maimonides in his early life did not believe most of the philosophy he later shaped and wrote leaving an everlasting study of a doctrinal creed for millions of Jews who follow it today. He authored the 13 Principles of Faith which traditional Jews live by even today. This is where the difference enters in between Jews and Christians; the twelve tenets of faith say, "The coming of the Jewish Messiah, "Hebrew

---

[12] http://en. Wikipedia.org/wiki/Israel Demographics of Israel

translation: "God's anointed." He strongly believed in the Gaonic, which means "pride" or "splendour" in Biblical Hebrew and since the 19th century, "genius" as in modern day Hebrew. Geonim, or the rabbis, played a prominent and decisive role in the transmission and teaching of Torah and Jewish Law. They taught Talmud and decided on issues on which no ruling had been rendered during the period of the Talmud.

There are two issues we must shed light upon here; (1) Jewish traditionalism, the majority of people in the promised land in modern-day Israel practice these 13 Principles of Faith, in particular number twelve. (2) The father of the Principles of Faith was a believer in North Africa version of faith principles, mainly monotheist. (One God) Now the issue to focus on is Maimonides took from the Africans originators what he wanted to use with the exception that Christ had come as the Messiah and the people no longer live under the "old covenant" of Mosaic Laws. The information he studied was from the Greek translation of the Torah and Hebrew texts, so he surely had benefit of the same information the earlier fathers of the gospels had. The text once again is abundantly clear in the Holy Bible; Isaiah 9:6 which cannot be refuted nor should be. We must journey back to scripture and examine what the promise to Abraham was and what it meant.

> "And the Lord said unto Abram, after that Lot was separated from him, Lift up thine eyes and look from the place where thou art northward, and southward, and eastward, and westward; For all the land thou seest, to thee will I give it, and to thy seed for ever." (Genesis 13:10) (KJV)

After Lot had been taken captive by the kings from Sodom and Gomorrah, the text says,

> "And there came one that had escaped, and told Abram the Hebrew...." (Genesis 14:13) (KJV)

This is the first mention of Abraham as a Hebrew. The title Hebrew is traceable to the Hebrew language which means, ah-var or "to pass-over." In other words he was being referred to as "the man from the region beyond." It was applied to Abraham because he crossed the Euphrates on his journey southwestward to the land of Canaan. The meaning has significance as the silence of the text would imply that Abraham was instructed by God to go to Canaan and as far as he would be able to see in any direction, he and his seed would possess the land "forever." God's promise is immutable. Therefore, the question looms all more important, are the modern day Jews, really the descendants of Abraham? There exist reservations about the identity of the modern-day Jew and his relationship to Abraham, Isaac and Jacob. For the majority of Christians the answer is a foregone conclusion if the believers who read and study the Holy Bible and believe its very word. The contention is that, if the Bible is the inspired word of God written by men, then it is to be believed. Ask this question of the average person claiming to be a Christian, and he/she will quickly tell you: The true descendants of Abraham, Isaac, and Jacob are those people today who call themselves Jews. Yet in light of that answer, we should know that the Bible makes it very clear that there are imposters masquerading as Israelites although no Israelite blood flows through their veins. The book of Revelation informs us of this deception and the identity of these blasphemers.

> "I know thy works and tribulation, and poverty, (but thou art rich) and I know the blasphemy of them which say they are Jews, and are not, but are the synagogue of Satan." (Revelation 2:9) (KJV)

If the occupiers of Israel are believers in the Jewish faith and not professed Christians believing in the Word of God (Bible) then they are not entitled to God's Covenant promise and thus are not entitled to the Promised Land. The facts we presented earlier regarding the population make-up of Israel points to the fact that the majority of the occupiers of the land are from Eastern Europe and/or are descendants of those people. Fast-forward to modern times, according to scripture, all Israeli occupants of the land should be from the descendants or seed of Abraham as well as from "the region beyond." The name "Jew" derives from the tribe of Judah and its descendants, which the most prominent seed is that of Emanuel, "God is with us," who by the way was born in (North Eastern Africa) and is from "the region." The principles are simple as one can see, if we are to believe the Bible, all of it, (not just portions) it is clear who the chosen people of God are and the region from which they would migrate from in masses rather than a paltry few. But the facts are quite telling, the masses or majority of occupiers of the "promise land," today come from an entirely different continent. God warned His people, that He would scatter them over the face of the earth if they were not obedient. He first did this with the Babylon exile which then led to the Diaspora in which most exiled Jews did not return home but stayed in Babylon or migrated to other places.

"And when He had come near, He beheld the city, and wept over it. Saying, if thou hadst known, even thou at least in this thy day, the things which belong unto thy peace! But now they are hid from thine eyes. For the days shall come upon thee, that thine enemies shall cast a trench about thee, and compass thee round, and keep thee in on every side. And shall lay thee even with the ground and thy children with thee; and they shall not leave in thee one stone upon another; because thou knewest not the time of thy visitation." (Luke 19:41-44) (KJV)

"But before all these, they shall lay their hands on you, and persecute you, delivering you up to the synagogues and into prisons, being brought before kings and rulers for my name's sake." (Luke 21:12) (KJV)

Following Christ's warning that God's judgment was about to fall again, the Jews were almost totally removed from Israel and scattered over North Africa and Southern Europe. Of course Jesus was foretelling the destruction of Jerusalem in A.D. 70 by the Romans. He foretold things regarding the persecution of Christians and dispersion of Jews to all parts of the earth until the end of the times of the Gentiles at the second coming of Christ. The 13 Principles of Faith, especially the twelve tenet, written by Maimonides some thousand years later, is well, inaccurate. Jesus said,

"And ye shall be betrayed both by parents, and brethren, and kinsfolks, and friends; and some of you shall they cause to be put to death. And ye shall be hated of all men for my name's sake." (Luke 21:16-17) (KJV)

At the time of the Hearing of the Word, to most it was almost inconceivable, yet it pictured the power of demon religions in their control of their victims. Religion caused the first betrayal and death and it will cause the last ones. The false religions have caused men to commit every known crime and the lowest of deeds while at the same time it made them think they were serving God and their inhuman deeds were righteous. As an example of this prediction by Christ, the rise of the Catholic Church for one brought a horrible and hounding persecution of the Jews wherever they fled, fulfilling God's curse. "And ye shall be hated of all men for my name's sake," as anti-Semitism was (blood descendants of Shem and Abraham) revived to new heights. Never was religion introduced to the Jews under more repulsive predictions. Concerning these predictions by the founder of Christianity, if one believes that He has not come yet as the "Messiah," how could they believe that they are the "chosen people," and are entitled to inherit the promise and the land? The success of Christianity, gives way to the proof of its Divine Origin and founder Jesus. Let me pause here to say, I am using fact specific narrative and quoting facts from the Holy Bible and factual doctrine as written in the 13 Principles of Faith, for Jewish believers.

Chapter 5

IDENTITY THEFT

Persecution eventually forced the Israelite Jews to migrate to Eastern Europe and Western Russia where they met and intermarried with the non-Israelite Khazar Jews. The Jewish Encyclopedia promotes the following concerning these people of Turkish origins. Their lives are woven in with the beginnings of the history of the Jews of Russia. The Czars of Russia renewed the persecution which forced the Jews to immigrate to other areas of the world. Eastern European Jews were of the Khazar bloodline, rather than the Abrahamic bloodline. It occurred during the 9th and 10th century under the rule of a king named Obadiah, who regenerated the kingdom and strengthened the Jewish religion. He took upon himself to invite various Jewish scholars to settle within his dominions and they in turn founded synagogues and schools. The writings are taken from Arabic and Slavonian sources that the religious disputation at the Chazarian court is a well-known historical fact. The map illustration from the Jewish Encyclopedia clearly illustrates the Jew's position regarding their ancestry.[13] (Illustration Map No. 6) It is said that some say their genetic lineage is primarily from the Turkish/Mongolian Khazars rather than from the lineage of Abraham, Isaac and Jacob. It would have been during the 7th and 9th centuries this all evolved as the adopting of Judaism. According to the Jewish Encyclopedia this conversion gave rise to their false claim of being Judahites when by mere fact they would have no right, historically or racially.

The modern-day descendants (majority Israelies) claim to being Jews is strictly religious. This information is corroborated under the heading "Khazars" in The New Standard Jewish Encyclopedia. Khazars; a Turkish tribe which settled in the lower Volga region sometime during the 8th century, a powerful Judaizing movement manifested itself among the Khazars. Ultimately, about 786-809, their king Bulan and 4,000 of his nobles accepted Judaism, the prince Obadiah being

---

[13] The Jewish Encyclopedia

active in securing their Judaization.[14] If they were not of this bloodline then they could not be Semites. If they are not Semites, then anyone who wrongly persecuted them could not be rightly labeled anti-Semitic or anti-bloodline of Shem and Abraham. The Bible makes it clear that Shem was the ancestor of the people of the ancient near east generally and the Hebrews specifically. In Luke, the apostle outlines the lineage of Jesus backwards all the way back to Adam. Apostle Matthew moves forward from Abraham to Joseph. Luke's entire section from Joseph to David differs dramatically from that given by Matthew. Luke's message is seen as Mary's genealogy and Matthew's version represents Joseph's. Thus the royal line is passed through Jesus' legal/royal record father and his physical descent from David is established by Mary's lineage as natural/royal record. While on the cross, this explains why Jesus gave Mary the son in John that she never really had of Shem through Abraham. The previous narrative is deemed necessary because it points to the fact that Jesus and Abraham came from the same lineage as Shem and Abraham who was the first Hebrew, which makes Jesus in reality a Hebrew first by bloodline or Semitic (bloodline of Shem and

---

[14] The New Standard Jewish Encyclopedia Doubleday and Company, Inc. Garden City, New York 1977 page 1132

Abraham) Author/Evangelist, Mr. Ted R. Weiland, writes in his book, God's Covenant People, "Mostly third party and circumstantial evidence in a convincing way conclude the East European Jews were not Semites (blood descendants of Shem and Abraham). Since they are not Semites, then today's Jews certainly cannot be of Abraham's lineage because Abraham was a Semite, descended from Shem, the Son of Noah.

Following the same line of reasoning, since today's Jews are not Semites, they cannot be Israelites either because Jacob/Israel was also a Semite, a direct descendant of Shem through Abraham."[15] In other words there are those who claim to be of the house of Judah or Judahites and therefore Israelites, but who are in reality imposters identified by Yeshua as a synagogue of Satan. They are in affect killing off or have non-suited the original people and disenfranchised them of their birthrights as well as the Promised Land. (Canaan) There is a double explanation in the scriptures.

> "Behold, I will make them of the synagogue of Satan, which say they are Jews, and are not, but do lie; behold, I will make them to come and worship before thy

---

[15] God's Covenant People

feet, and to know that I have loved thee."
(Revelation 3:9) (KJV)

Most Jews are of the opinion that Jesus was
Semitic but hailed from the Middle East. They
refuse to acknowledge the fact that He was born
in Northeastern Africa by calling this region the
Middle East. Is that reason enough then to make
Jesus any less Black? Jewish author Arthur
Koestler, stated in his book "The Thirteenth
Tribe," that the true ancestry of today's Jewish
people; genetically they are more closely related
to the Hun, Uigar and Magyar tribes than to the
seed of Abraham, Isaac and Jacob. If this is the
case, his opinion is the term "anti-Semitism"
would become void of all meaning. He further
states that the Khazars and their King are all
Jews yet not genetically, but rather by
conversion to Judaism. He points out in
scripture that they (Khazars) may be that of Gog
and Magog.

> "Princes shall come out of Egypt; Ethiopia
> shall soon stretch out her hands unto God."
> (Psalm 68:31) (KJV)

> "From beyond the rivers of Ethiopia my
> supplants, even the daughter of my
> dispersed, shall bring mine that, the
> offering." (Zephaniah 3:10) (KJV)

We've already seen that God said "Out of
Egypt, I have called my son,"

The African/Edenic Hebrews will return back to Israel (Canaan) from the lands beyond the Nile. God said to His people; I Will gather, I Will deal, I Will Save, I Will appoint, I Will bring you back, I Will give you. There are two distinct groups of Jews in the world and they come from two different areas of the world. The Sephardic Jews are from the Middle East (Northeastern Africa) and the Ashkenazi Jews, which come from Eastern Europe. The first mentioned group is the oldest and they are the Jews described in the Bible as they lived in the area. Oh by the way, they are blood cousins of the Arabs and the only real difference between them is religion. Surprising enough, as we take our point to its conclusion, 90% of the world's Jews are Askenazi who had a very strange beginning. They came into existence about 1200 years ago approximately in or during the 8th century A.D.[16] The final source reference we implore in this narrative is by Mr. Wilmot Robertson, who states in his book The Dispossessed Majority, that the non-Israelite Jews in Slavic lands, the Ashkenazim, are to be distinguished from the Sephardim, the purer-blooded Mediterranean Jews. The Zionist pioneers of Palestine were mostly Ashkenazim,

---

[16] Jack Bernstein, as told by Len Martin in *The Life of An American Jew in Racist Marxist Israel* The Noontide Press 1984 page 6

the "un-Jewish" temperament and character of these Zionists were accented by their "un-Jewish" appearance.[17]

We began by stating that "there is nothing new under the sun." Mr. Leo Heiman, who writes for the Coplan News Service in Tel Aviv, says Nathan Pollack has a beef with the Israeli government. Mr. Pollack migrated from Poland some 43 years ago and wanted to celebrate the Jewish Khazar 1000th anniversary alliance which the government rejected. Coming from Russia, Mr. Pollack is a translator of scientific texts and proofreader in a publishing firm. In conclusion of this diatribe with the same notation, suffice to say, we strongly believe there is a purpose under Heaven and after more than two-thousand years the prophecy is being fulfilled that Egypt shall be restored and that Ethiopia, shall stretch out her hand. The African/Edenic Hebrews rather than the occupiers of the Promised Land are indeed God's first fruits, His sons and daughters the original "burnt –faced" people descendants of Abraham, Ham and Shem have been without doubt duped, denied, identity stolen and criminally treated by non-Christian zealots who have never believed the Messiah came, died for

---

[17] The Dispossessed Majority, Wilmot Robertson Cape Canaveral, Fl; Howard Enterprises, 1972 page 156

our sins, was resurrected that we might be reconciled back unto a right relationship with God and prepare the Kingdom of God for His return to Rapture His church to be with Him in eternity. The facts are documented for all who will read and receive the hearing of the Word, the coming unto one's own knowledge and not of man's ideological depraved banter which has set the world teetering on the brink of Armageddon. We cast no dispersion upon anyone or any group of culture-minded people for after all, many of these people have lived with these cultural beliefs all their lives and have handed these false notions from one generation to the next perpetuating the "Great Lie." We don't apologize for uncovering T.R.U.T.H. (Thought, Revelations, Understanding, Tarry, Holy Spirit) as we find it through research and countless hours of reading and studying texts and journals of which many, are written by Jewish authors. The truth cannot be bottled- up, corked and placed out to sea to float away into perpetuity, no it must be told.

Chapter 6

Birth of Emmanuel

Isaiah derives its title from the author, whose name means, "The Lord is salvation," and is similar to the names Joshua, Elisha and Jesus. Isaiah is quoted directly in the New Testament over sixty-five times, which is far more than any other Old Testament prophet and is mentioned by his name over twenty times. The son of Amoz, he ministered in and around Jerusalem as prophet to Judah during the reigns of four kings of Judah; Uzziah, Jotham, Ahaz and Hezekiah. Early church father Jerome likened him to Demosthenes, the legendary Greek orator. He was a contemporary of Hosea and Micah and it is held in tradition that he met his death under King Manasseh by being cut in two with a wooden saw.

> "They were stoned, they were sawn asunder, were tempted, were slain with the

sword; they wandered about in sheepskins and goatskins; being destitute, afflicted, tormented; of whom the world was not worthy they wandered in deserts and mountains and in dens and caves of the earth. And these all having obtained a good report through faith, received not the promise. God having provided some better thing for us that they without us should not be made perfect." (Hebrew 11:37-40) (KJV)

Isaiah writings feature a range of 2,186 different words, compared to 1,535 in Ezekiel, 1,653 in Jeremiah and 2,170 in the Psalms. II Chronicles 32:32 records that he wrote a biography of King Hezekiah. The prophet lived until at least 681 B.C. Fulfillment of some of his prophecies in his own lifetime provided his credentials for the prophetic office. The key fulfillment of his prophecy of Christ first coming, have given Isaiah further vindication for all those who doubted his reality based prophetic utterances concerning Christ. Isaiah provides future Day of The Lord and the time following. He details numerous aspects of Israel's future kingdom on earth not found elsewhere in the Old or New Testament, including changes in nature, the animal world, Jerusalem's status among the nations and the Suffering Servant's leadership. What is found at the crux of his prophetic renderings is "foreshortening." Here the prophet predicted future events without delineating exact sequences of the events or time intervals separating them. For example, nothing in Isaiah reveals the extended period separating the two comings of the Messiah. Also he does not provide as clear a distinction between the future temporal kingdom and the eternal kingdom as John does in Revelation. In God's program of progressive revelation, details of these relationships awaited a prophetic spokesman in a later time. Known also as the "evangelical prophet," he spoke much about the grace of God toward Israel, particularly within the last twenty-seven chapters of his writings. Many see the centerpiece of his writings in the fifty-third chapter, portraying Christ as the slain Lamb of God.

As the prophet uttered some of his most famous prophetic impartations, Christians generally hold that Immanuel as described in Isaiah 7:14 cannot be an ideal or metaphorical person, and cannot be identified with the regenerate people of Israel, nor with religious faith, for "he shall eat butter and honey." (Isaiah 7:15) It is misunderstood that both the text and the context indicate that the Prophet does not refer to a child in general, but points to an individual. In particular he gives the prophecy to King Ahaz as a sign that the two kings he dreads, Rezin king of Damascus and Pekah king of Samaria will shortly be destroyed by the king of Assyria when Immanuel is still an infant. Christians and Jews alike differ amongst themselves that the name Immanuel refers to a son to be born of either Isaiah or Ahaz, in which case perhaps the future royal heir Hezekiah son. As well there are those who believe that Immanuel cannot be Jesus either, for three reasons, the first being the angels who spoke to Mary did not say he would be called Immanuel, secondly he was named Jesus by his parents, and finally because in Isaiah 9:6 it is said that "... His name will be called Wonderful Counselor, Mighty God, Eternal Father, Prince of Peace." However, it is clear that Matthew believed Jesus to be the ultimate fulfillment of such prophecy as "God with us" or "Immanuel." In Matthew "an angel of the Lord" appears to Mary's betrothed husband Joseph in a dream and tells him:

> "And she shall bring forth a son, and thou shalt call his name Jesus: for he shall save his people from their sins." (Matthew 1:21) (KJV)

The text continues with the comment:

> "All this happened to fulfill what the Lord had spoken by the prophet." (Matthew 1:22) (KJV)

> "Behold, a virgin shall be with child, and shall bring forth a son and they shall call

his name Emmanuel, which being interpreted is, God with us." (Matthew 1:23) (KJV)

Some 5th and 6th century manuscripts of the Gospel according to Matthew read Isaiah the prophet instead of merely "the prophet." This however, does not have the support of other important witnesses. Rather than using the Masoretic text which forms the basis of most modern Christian Old Testament translations, Matthew's quotation is taken from the Septuagint. The verb "I call" is used by both Isaiah and Gabriel; but while the former employs the third person plural "thou shalt call," the latter has the second person singular "you shall call." Gabriel himself therefore is not applying Isaiah's prophecy to Joseph, but his purpose is to instruct him to assume legal paternity of the son to be born of Mary by naming him. It is the following comment that explains Mary's conception by the Holy Spirit, Joseph's vocation as the child's legal father, and the child's own vocation as the Saviour of his people as indicated by the name Jesus, in the light of Isaiah's prophecy that henceforth "God is with us". Here there can be no misunderstanding of Immanuel's identity; otherwise there would not have been a need for the angel Gabriel to convey the message to Joseph. Again, this is an instance where one either believes in the written Logos or not. It should not be used as a tool of confusion or mis-information for one to take some truths and promote and, leave others to be questioned by man's thoughts. Judaism understands the passages in Isaiah literally as referring to a child born during the reign of king Ahaz to whom the prophecy was made and does not consider the verses to be connected with the Messiah.

Rabbi Naftali Silberberg, writes his opinion of just why Jews don't believe Jesus was the Messiah. He writes, Maimonides writes (Laws of Kings 11:4) the criteria for identifying the messiah: "If a king will arise from the House of David, diligent in Torah study and the fulfillment of mitzvahs- of the written and oral law- like David his ancestor, and will compel all the Jews to go in its (the Torah's) path and builds the Holy Temple and gathers the Diaspora (to the land of Israel), this is certainly the Messiah." Jesus did not fulfill any of the basic duties of the Messiah he says and additionally, the Bible is replete with prophecies about the Messianic Era (see for example Isaiah 11) which were never realized. He goes on to write; to put it in simple words; if Jesus is the Messiah and this is what Redemption is all about- who needs the Messiah? The Messiah I await will fulfill all the promises of world peace and global monotheism which are vividly described by the prophets.[18] Rabbi Silberberg, is a native of Detroit, Michigan and a renowned scholar known for his sharp wit and vast Talmudic knowledge. He currently resides in Brooklyn, New York with his wife and their three children. What can be ascertained from Rabbi Silberberg is the fact that he is an astute scholar when it comes to Talmud writings and how to apply them to those who are of the Jewish faith. The problem is, he along with others do not believe in the message of Christ or that he was the Messiah and that He was resurrected from the dead, thus they are not Christians. They are guided by the "Law" and believe that the Messiah is coming and that Jesus had to have been a prophet. The problem with this is, he like most Jews denies the scripture when it says,

> "Think not that I Am come to destroy the law, or the prophets: I Am not come to destroy, but to fulfill. For verily I say unto you, Till heaven and earth pass, one jot or one tittle shall in no wise pass from the law, till all be fulfilled." (Matthew 5:17-18) (KJV)

---

[18] http://www.askmoses.com

Isaiah is saying what thus said the Lord;

"Incline your ear and come unto me; hear, and your soul shall live; and I will make an everlasting covenant with you, even the sure mercies of David." (Isaiah 55:3) (KJV)

We see by this text that God is bound by His own Word to fulfill the promises He has made to bring His people back unto Himself and bless them in that future day. God promises the kingdom to David and the church to the people, not Israel. The church which Christ founded, are the people bonded together in,

"....the unity of the bond of peace." In other words, one may say that is the real Israel. Apostle Paul said "There is one body, and one Spirit, even as ye are called in one hope of your calling. One Lord, one faith, one baptism. One God and Father of all, who is above all, and through all, and in you all. But unto every one of us is given grace according to the measure of the gift of Christ." (Ephesians 4:3-7)

So what I gain from that scripture is meaningful in the sense that Jesus did fulfill prophecies written by Isaiah. Paul, who was an astute student of the "law" was even convinced that Jesus lived, died and was resurrected to the glory of God and that He gifted unto all men the grace which surpasses all understanding, even in the understanding he possessed, that of mastery of the Talmudic laws. I concur with Rabbi Silberberg being a scholar of Talmudic Law, however, when it comes to Jesus, he falls short of the glory that dwelled in Him and the message He gave to the world. As the Rabbi points out, prophecies which never came to pass according to his understanding in Isaiah 11 for example says;

> "And He shall set up an ensign for the nations, and shall assemble the outcasts of Israel, and gather together the dispersed of Judah from the four corners of the earth."
> (Isaiah 11:12) (KJV)

The text says, "He will set-up an ensign for the nations," this means a standard or symbol. The Bible does not describe Israel's official standard; so we have no idea of its appearance.[19] If the written Logos does not give a description of the Standard (Ensign) of Israel, this would mean that the time has not yet come for this prophecy to be fulfilled. Surely, if God said it would happen, I believe that it will, but only in God's time not mans'. To his credit he does not mention Ezekiel, but we are, because it points to the fact that we are now living in that

---

[19] Nelson's Illustrated Bible Dictionary Thomas Nelson Publishers, Standard; defined as Ensign page 1010

dispensation of God's time which the prophet spoke of in this writing;

> "And there shall be no more a pricking brier unto the house of Israel, nor any grieving thorn of all that are round about them, that despised them; and they shall know that I am the Lord God. Thus saith the Lord God; when I shall have gathered the house of Israel from the people among whom they are scattered, and shall be sanctified in them in the sight of the heathen, then shall they dwell in their land that I have given to my servant Jacob. And they shall dwell safely therein and shall build houses and plant vineyards; yea they shall dwell with confidence, when I have executed judgments upon all those that despise them round about them and they shall know that I am the Lord their God." (Ezekiel 28:24-26) (KJV)

One must wonder why the state of Israel have never lived or existed in peace and safety. Did God gather a people from a foreign land and give them a promise they were not entitled to? Why is it that the majority of the Israeli population does not believe in Jesus as the Messiah? Why can't they dwell safely in the land which God gave to His servant Jacob (Canaan?) These questions derive from the text of the prophet Ezekiel upon reading. Could the answer to the above questions be because, the occupiers of the land are not the chosen people and until the chosen people of God are gathered and brought to their land of inheritance there indeed will be no safe dwelling. Until God executes judgment upon those that despise them, which in a multitude of cases are the chosen heirs? I place this discussion on the table of scholars and debaters to help resolve these all important issues. In the interim, we believe in the inspired word of God from the Holy Bible and thus stand on the word that Jesus came, sacrificed His blood that all men might be able to receive the gift of salvation and He was buried and rose again to fulfill the scriptures written by the prophets of the Old Testament.

> "Now is my soul troubled; and what shall I say? Father, save me from this hour: but for this cause came I unto this hour. Father Glorify thy name. Then came there a voice from heaven, saying, I have glorified it, and will glorify it again. The people that stood by, and heard it said that it thundered; others said, an angel spake to him. Jesus answered and said, this voice came not because of me, but for your sakes. Now is the judgment of this world; now shall the prince of this world be cast out. And if I be lifted up from the earth, will draw all men unto me." (John12:27-32) (KJV)

Chapter 7

Doctrinal Message

The definition of "doctrine," is simply a body of beliefs about God, man, Christ, the church and various other related concepts considered authoritative and thus worthy of acceptance by members of the community of faith. As we dialogue here concerning doctrinal message, we will explore the tone that was set by the message of Christ which he taught and ministered to humanity for the purpose of showing men how God expected them to lead their lives in accordance with His statutes and commandants. Christ condemned the doctrine of the Pharisees because it was of human origin. By contrast, Jesus' teaching was not systematic and repetitious, yet it carried a refreshing tone of reconciliation in the hopes of bringing humanity back nigh God's dwelling. In order to accomplish this feat Jesus knew he had to destroy the yoke of bondage the Pharisees had over the people by first exposing, revealing and articulating the truths they would learn from the hearing of His Word. God's overall plan and purpose was showing through His teaching by revealing that Jesus was half man and half divinity. He said things which made common sense and sounded of human extract as well as verbalizing those things which were of a very divine nature. Thus the masters of Israel saw him in that sense as blaspheming God and other times they just wondered in amazement of his knowledge of heavenly things of which they themselves knew not. Hence they refuted the fact of him being identified as the Son of God and rejected out of hand the notion that he was the long awaited Messiah. Even today, the doctrinal message of Judaism will not acknowledge the facts of what the ancient ones bore witness to on the hill at Calvary. Their texts do not speak of the graves opening up and the dead walking through the streets of Jerusalem, or of the empty tomb though it was guarded and the stone still in place.

> "And the graves were opened; and many bodies of the saints which slept arose, and came out of the graves after his resurrection, and went into the Holy city, and appeared unto many." (Matthew 27:52-53) (KJV)

It was so unbelievable to them that they paid a king's ransom to the guards to tell Pilate that Jesus followers came by night and stole his remains away, not even bothering to acknowledge the fact that his grave clothes were still in place undisturbed as if there was still a body contained in and under the linen garments.

> "Pilate said unto them, Ye have a watch; go your way, make it as sure as ye can. So they went, and made the sepulcher sure, sealing the stone and setting the watch." (Matthew 27:65-66)

> "Now when they were going, behold, some of the watch came into the city, and showed unto the chief priests all the things that were done. And when they were assembled with the elders, and had taken counsel, they gave large money unto the soldiers. Saying, Say ye, His disciples came by night, and stole him away while we slept. And if this comes to the governor's ears, we will persuade him, and secure you. So they took the money, and did as they were taught: and this saying is commonly reported among the Jews until this day." (Matthew 28: 11-15) (KJV)

In the early development of Christianity, many African people can say they played an important role in this movement. The crossroads of this early development were established long before the Gospel reached the shores of Europe and Asia. Christ birth took place on and within the fertile lands of Mother Africa and we must prompt the world to understand that He was a brown-skinned Semite and he probably resembled the present-day dark complexioned Yemenite Jews. Contrary to popular beliefs which in many circles view the Jewish religion as being practiced only by a restricted ethnic group, this in fact, couldn't be further than from the truth. It is acknowledged throughout some scholarly enclaves that both before and after the time of Christ, there were black Africans who were Jews. After all, Moses married a black woman and there were frequent visits of black people to Jerusalem as pilgrims. The Jewish influence among certain tribes of West Africa and the very existence of the Falashas or "black Jews" of Ethiopia tend to crystallize this conception of historical ideals and pertinent facts. Philip the evangelist was guided by the Holy Spirit in his encounter with the eunuch,

> "And Philip ran thither to him and heard him read the prophet Esaias, and said, Understandest thou what thou readest?" (Acts 8:30) (KJV)

The eunuch was an Ethiopian of authoritative status. This passage has great historical value for it was in the first century A.D. these events took place again visiting the factual thoughts of Ethiopia being Christian many years prior to the European. Many Europeans have had great difficulty acknowledging the Ethiopian's baptism as bona fide, since the text only mentions a water baptism without referencing the descent of the Holy Spirit. In short one can only stand in utter amazement at the diverse lengths at which some Christian scholars and religious leaders have gone to vent their narrow mindsets in truly understanding the text. It sort of relates to "lean not unto thine own understanding." The eunuch first of all in analysis, was a learned man who was reading the Hebrew text of Isaiah (Esaias) suggesting what is really happening is perhaps a Ethiopian Jew who undoubtedly understands what he is reading and is indeed open-minded to a deeper new interpretation.

> "And the eunuch answered Philip, and said, I pray thee, of whom speaketh the prophet this? Of himself, or of some other man? Then Philip opened his mouth, and began at the same scripture, and preached unto him Jesus." (Acts 8:34-35) (KJV)

> "And Philip said, If thou believest with all thine heart, thou mayest. And he answered and said, I believe that Jesus Christ is the Son of God." (Act 8:37) (KJV)

A very important note we must remember here, all this occurred before the Apostle Paul was converted on the road to Damascus. And who was this Saul? He was a Pharisees who was learned in the way of the Talmudic Law and was relentlessly persecuting these new Christians who were following and believing the message and teachings of the Messiah.

Jesus' message today is the same as he gave to those who followed him while He was on earth. His messages were recorded for us today as if he knew what our needs were going to be. The human side of Christ was, he did know full well what our needs, worries, situations and healing processes would be. After all His divine nature gave Him great insight of all things that were before and those things which were to come. During the time the Apostle John was called to heaven, Jesus told him to write these things down for the time is at hand. God through His most renowned emissary was absolute, unlimited and intrinsically part of His eternal nature and being. His everlasting Word of

> "I am the first and the last: I am he that liveth, and was dead; and, behold, I am alive for evermore, Amen and have the keys of hell and of death." (Revelation 1:17-18) (KJV)

God created us in His own image so we can know Him personally and have a joy-filled life. He created us not as robots to automatically love and obey Him, but gave us a will and a freedom of choice. Since the beginning of time, we have chosen to disobey God and go our own willful way. We still make this choice today. This results in separation from God and ends in misery. So herein here lies, the real message from Christ, be obedient and God will bless us as far as we can "see." My spiritual father Bishop Larry D. Trotter wrote in his book Living Above See Level, "Faith stands as the answer to all of your questions, the truth to every lie, and the direction to every pathway. I implore you to learn to live where you want to be, not simply where you are now. This requires vision, start working toward your tomorrow, today." This is the direct message from Jesus, "God will and can bless you so far beyond your wildest dreams that it will literally blow your mind....You have the ability to live above SEE level...."[20]

---

[20] Living Above See Level, Larry D. Trotter, Mark One ;A division of KDR Consulting, LLC pages 116 and 117

Chapter 8

INFANCY OF CHRISTIANITY

It is only fitting that we begin this section with an African early church father named Tertullian. From the beginning of the third century he inaugurated Christian literature in the Latin language. Through him the practice of theology was in Latin, Tertullian's works brought decisive benefits which would be unforgivable to underestimate. According to some of the writings of Pope Benedict XVI, Tertullian's influence covered different areas; linguistically and the use of classical culture to single out a common "Christian soul" in the world and in the formulation of new proposals of human coexistence.[21] In reading some of the works of Tertullian one receives the express

---

[21] Pope Benedict XVI Church Fathers; from Clement of Rome to Augustine; Ignatius Press, San Francisco 2008 by Libreria Editrice Vaticana, Vatican City

idea that he was with the plan of Salvation for God's people and did his best to teach those who were his followers how best they might gather some of the same knowledge and wisdom he possessed. So as we begin this narrative we must go back to the beginning after the death of Christ. The Christian movement probably began not from a single center but from many different centers where different groups of disciples of Jesus gathered and tried to make sense of what they had experienced with him and what had happened to him at the end of his public ministry. Each of those groups probably had a very different take on what the significance of Jesus was. Some of them understood his death and the resurrection experience, from the point of view of them focusing on it, in terms of exaltation. Others may understand it in terms of a resuscitation of the corpse of Jesus, others not worrying very much at all about the resurrection of Jesus, but concentrating on his teaching and trying to disseminate that. We can see, even in the canonical text, in the Book of Acts, there were different groups that were in competition with one another. Those who insisted more strongly on observance of Jewish laws in the Torah competed with those who were more open to admission of gentiles without important and current religious authorities to regain the hearts and minds of the people. After all, whoever had control of the minds of the people, truly controlled the masses. The Pharisees really had this one down unto their own understanding. They wouldn't allow the people to worship a man who they believed was a mere prophet and certainly not the Son of God. They did not want him referred to as the King of the Jews either.

> "And Pilate wrote a title, and put it on the cross. And the writing was, Jesus of Nazareth The King Of The Jews. This title then read many of the Jews: for the place where Jesus was crucified was nigh to the city; and it was written in Hebrew and Greek and Latin. Then said the chief priests of the Jews to Pilate, Write not, The King of The Jews; but that he said, I am King of the Jews. Pilate answered, What I have written I have written." (John19:19-22) (KJV)

In their small minds this was a blasphemous misnomer which was to be corrected by strict observance of the law and guiding the people in reverse, back to Talmudic laws. There were others who we meet again in the Book of Acts, who apparently stood in continuity with the activity of John the Baptist and did not know the baptism that the Pauline Christians, at least, knew. So there was much more diversity in the early stages of the Christian movement than the Book of Acts suggest.

Christianity, or one would rather say "Christianities," of the second and third centuries were a highly variegated phenomenon. We really can't imagine Christianity as a unified coherent religious movement. Certainly there were some religious organizations. There were institutions developing in some Christian churches, but only in some. And this was not universal by any means. We know, for example, the literature recovered at Nag Hammadi, that Gnostic Christianity didn't have the kind of clear hierarchy that other forms of Christianity had developed. They still clung to a charismatic leadership model. In doing so, there were a lot of variety in second (2nd) and third (3rd) century Christianity. They called into question the values of civilized society and instead fostered spiritual values and life-styles which were to some, of a radical nature. Some of these radical Gnostics apparently retreated from the world to the solitary life of the monk or the ascetic and outright refused to participate in the everyday business of human society. The discovery of the Nag Hammadi texts have somewhat served to refute the hostile writings of philosophers and theologians who tried to silence the Gnostics to speak for themselves and present their faith and theology in a fair and attractive manner. The compositions of the "spectacular documents," from the Nag Hammadi are published in volume: The Secret

Book of James, The Gospel of Thomas, The
Book of Thomas and The Secret Book of John.
Of the four, two are classics of Gnostics
spirituality, known also from other manuscripts
or fragments of manuscripts. Although the
precise dating of ancient documents is
notoriously difficult, all four of these texts seem
to have been written around the 2nd century
C.E., the Secret Book of James and the Gospel
of Thomas probably being earlier than the Book
of Thomas and the Secret Book of John.[22]

One of the facts revealed in the Hag
Hammadi texts is contained in the Secret Book
of James. He is sending a secret book revealed
to himself and Peter by the Lord. He says that
he wrote it in Hebrew and considering that you
are a minister for the salvation of the saints will
try to be careful not to communicate this book
to many people, for the Savior did not even
want to communicate it to all of us, his twelve
disciples. Nonetheless, blessed are those who
will be saved through the faith of this treatise.
The significance here is that as the disciples
were gathered writing their fond memories of
Jesus, he appeared. It had been five hundred
days after he arose from the dead, we said to

---

[22] The Secret Teachings of Jesus; Four Gnostic Gospels
Translated by Marvin W. Meyer Publisher Random House,
Inc. New York pages introduction xvii & xviii

him, "Did you depart and leave us?" Jesus said, "No, but I shall return to the place from which I came. If you wish to come with me, come!" One can detect the fear in the voice of James, the fear of knowing that their Savior was dead yet He lives again and has appeared to them once again to give them words of exhortation and encouragement that they might be able to carry on even in the face of hostility from the Pharisees who as we read in John 19, were convinced that Jesus was not the King of the Jews nor any such thing as royalty or high priesthood, moreover to be referred to as Child of Humanity.[23] This small sample of writings from some 2000 years ago, serves as a sure purpose for why I for one, do not believe in theology.

> "A fool hath no delight in understanding but in expressing his own heart." (Proverbs 18:2) (KJV)

If we remember to carefully study God's word that we might be able to avoid misinterpretation it will open our eyes revealing what God really has to say rather than what we already think. In the bigger scheme of things,

---

[23] The Secret Teachings of Jesus Four Gnostic Gospels Translated by Marvin W. Meyer Publisher Random House Inc. New York; Secret Book of James codex 1, pages 1-2 pages 2-3 chapter 1:2-11 chapter 2:4

what we think means nothing, for if we miss God it is all for naught anyway. The Pharisees of that era missed God and the opportunity He attempted to give to them and humanity at-large, that of Salvation and Grace of which through Him the world might be saved. It is the message Jesus brought forth through love and mercy in the affairs of the world over which He is Lord. He attempted to bring a renewing of human life, giving it heavenly quality and hope; it was a word that includes the entire spectrum of both the natural world as well as human civilization. And how did the religious leaders, the masters of Israel, the ones who the people looked up to, treat Jesus and his message? Without doubt, with disdain, humiliating Him and denouncing Him as a fraud, even unto this day. The Jewish beliefs are what they are, handed down through centuries of misinformation. The Bible teaches us that without knowledge the people will perish.

> "My people are destroyed for lack of knowledge; because thou hast rejected knowledge. I will also reject thee, that thou shalt be no priest to me: seeing thou hast forgotten the law of thy God. I will also forget thy children." (Hosea 4:6) (KJV)

Now like then the lack of knowledge has suffered unto the people causing them to lack knowledge of their cultural traditions. I'm referring to the Euro-Gentile reign over God's first fruits, not because of the Euro-Gentiles' greatness, but due to the lack of knowledge. Permit this writer to dwell here for a moment; much of the Bible was written by African men Apostles John **(Galilee)**, Matthew **(Palestine)**, Luke **(Syria)** and Prophets Moses **(Egypt)**, Isaiah **(Judah)**, and Daniel **(Jerusalem)**. All these lands comprised ancient Africa who because of their disobedience and violations of the laws and statutes, lost favor with God. As a result, they yielded the rule or dominion of the world to them, for an appointed period of time. It is my belief that these things shall come to pass whereby God's chosen people will return to their rightful places and once again enjoy the, "Light of the Son."

It was during the festival of Pentecost that the small band of disciples were transformed people speaking the Good News of God to fellow Jewish pilgrims from around the ancient world in their own native languages. After which, 3000 were converted to Christ and baptized on that day alone. The coming of the Holy Spirit was a watershed moment on that day because according to the Old Testament prophet Joel, his utterances were finally coming to pass.

"And it shall come to pass afterward, that I will pour out my spirit upon all flesh; and your sons and your daughters shall prophesy, your old men shall dream dreams, your young men shall see visions. And also upon the servants and upon the handmaids in those days will I pour out my spirit. And I will show wonders in the heavens and in the earth, blood and fire and pillars of smoke. The sun shall be turned into darkness and the moon into blood, before the great and the terrible day of the Lord come. And it shall come to pass, that whosoever shall call on the name of the Lord shall be delivered: for in mount Zion and in Jerusalem shall be deliverance, as the Lord hath said, and in the remnant whom the Lord shall call." (Joel 2:28-32) (KJV)

Now this must be exampled the true work of the cross written in some New Testament texts state, Jesus was the Word made flesh (John 1:14), and "The Word was God," (John 1:1) for in other texts of the New Testament, it is written;

"And Jesus said, for judgment I am come into this world, that they which see not might see; and that they which see might be made blind. And some of the Pharisees which were with him heard these words, and said unto him, are we blind also?" (John9:39-40) (KJV)

"Your father Abraham rejoiced to see my day; and he saw it, and was glad. Then said the Jews unto him; Thou art not yet fifty years old, and hast thou seen Abraham? Jesus said unto them, Verily, verily, I say unto you, before Abraham was, I am." (John8:56-58)

"And he is before all things, and by him all things consist, and he is the head of the body, the church; who is the beginning, the firstborn from the dead; that in all things he might have the preeminence. For it pleased the Father that in him should all fullness dwell." (Colossians 1:17-19)

Early church father Polycarp of Smyrna said, "Him who died for us, and for our sakes was raised again by God from the dead." [24]

Against all skepticism, Christians could now insist that truth is rooted in God's creation, existence and self-disclosures, rather than in human experience alone. God has become human in Jesus Christ, putting to flight the notion that humankind has no access to a transcendent word of truth. In Christ, God's

---

[24] Ante-Nicene Fathers Volume 1, Polycarp, Chapter IX. Letter to the Philippians. Edited by Alexander Roberts & James Donaldson American Edition, 1885

word was now made flesh. There was no mistaking Him for who he was anymore. The flesh had been crucified and the bloodshed in the ultimate sacrifice of which there were many who witnessed as well as those who witnessed and still refuse to believe. The New Testament message did not echo in a vacuum, nor did it encounter naïve persons who had never entertained religious or philosophical options. Their views rather clashed sometimes violently, with firmly established ideas and institutional movements such as the Pharisees. This came about because the old traditional Jewish customs or The Law was restored amongst the people in great measure by the priests for the sole purpose of no more than, stern control over the hearts and minds of the people. As the years went by other aspects of the people's lives were at best normal. They still worked their jobs, and went about their routine lives of raising families. However, this was not the case with those who sought after missionary work and service. For them herein began the early persecution due to their faith. This was not a deterrent then or now for they were never the same again after knowing Christ for themselves and believing the manifestation of His resurrection. The spread of the gospel got off to an early start with a boost through the thousands of worshipers converted on the Day of Pentecost. Upon returning to their perspective homes and synagogues in faraway places, they took with them word of Jesus, The Messiah. This would never leave room for doubt for many as the good news was spread rapidly. The core group of Jesus followers multiplied with an urgency like never seen before. This gospel of love, peace, healing, deliverance and freedom was a set of encouraging words never before heard emanating from the priests. There were many things the early Christians had in common with the Jews, however, with exception of the fact that the Jews believed the Messiah had yet to come and the new Christians believed with unwavering fear and conviction that He had come and had ascended back to the Father and now was interceding on the people's behalf with God. So quite naturally with these thoughts in mind, the people clearly no longer required the priests to make blood atonements for them anymore as they could go directly to God for themselves in repenting of their sins. These faithful followers of Christ's doctrine attempted to combine their former Jewish customs with what seemed appropriate to their new life in Christ. It became increasingly difficult to mesh and hold the two together. Early Christians in predominately Jewish Palestine continued to worship in the Jerusalem temple as well as synagogues. In addition to this approach, they pressed to meet in private homes for prayer, worship and study of scriptures and the apostles' teaching. There were cultural and even language differences with some speaking Aramaic or Hebrew and others speaking Greek. The murmurings in the church regarding work assignments had an air of contention and was problematic as human behavior would dictate. The Hebrews were the Aramaic- speaking Jews, while the Hellenists were the Greek-speaking Jews. It was a time of reevaluation as they sought to retain their ties with the past, yet sharpen their focus on what made them a new community of Christians. What was emerging from all this strife and tensions was the fact that the Christians ultimately were not a subset of any of the established sects of Judaism. In the reality of things, it was time for a parting of the ways. They believed that God had foretold the Christian movement in ancient prophecies and more recently in the preaching of John the Baptist and Jesus Himself. Jewish Christians felt that it was the non-Christians Jews who were abandoning their own ancient heritage by rejecting God's promised deliverer, Jesus of Nazareth, rose and exalted to God's right hand. They knew from scripture that the inclusion of the Gentiles among God's covenant people had long been prophesied. They felt they were fulfilling, not defying, the message of the Old Testament by the steps they took to adjust Jewish customs to the realities of non-Jewish communities. In their minds there absolutely could be no doubt of the essentials of Old Testament doctrine Jesus himself had observed, endorsed and elaborated in His own teachings. So of course with the traditional Jews not believing that Jesus was the Messiah, well, they weren't having any of this kind of talk and doctrinal teaching among the people and this is where the division of the Hebrews suffered its greatest schism, one that lasts even today.

The early Christians saw themselves as the people of God and inheritors of the Old Testament promises ushered in by the founder of this movement, Jesus Christ.

> "Have ye suffered so many things in vain? If it be yet in vain. He therefore that ministered to you the Spirit, and worketh miracles among you; doeth he it by the works of the law, or by the hearing of faith? Even as Abraham believed God, and it was accounted to him for righteousness. Know ye therefore that they which are of faith, the same are the children of Abraham. And the scripture, foreseeing that God would justify the heathen through faith, preached before the gospel unto Abraham saying, in thee shall all nations be blessed. So then they which be of faith are blessed with faithful Abraham. For as many as are of the works of the law are under the curse: for it is written, cursed is every one that continueth not in all things

which are written in the book of the law to do them. But that no man is justified by the law in the sight of God, it is evident: for, The just shall live by faith. And the law is not of faith: but, the man that doeth them shall live in them. Christ has redeemed us from the curse of the law, being made a curse for us: for it is written, cursed is every one that hangeth on a tree: That the blessing of Abraham might come on the Gentiles through Jesus Christ; that we might receive the promise of the Spirit through faith." (Galatians 3:4-14) (KJV)

Paul the apostle wrote these things inspired by God between 50-55 A.D., some twenty years after the death and ascension of Christ. He tried to serve as a buffer between the priests and the Christians as an expert of the laws. He attempted to warn them against legalism and defend justification by faith as well as invoking his apostolic authority. Oh if only the majority of the people had listened and reasoned with him, the world and its turmoil would certainly be a much better place in which to dwell. If we are to believe the scriptures, Paul used authority granted to him to give impartations into the earth realm to bring and draw God's people nigh unto God. Today as well as thousands' of years ago, it's not about power or filthy lucre, as it is more about controlling the hearts and minds of the people. The Christians and the

Jews fundamental difference centered especially around who Jesus was and what he had done. The Christians thoughts and position was simple, Jesus was God and became flesh and dwelled among the people. The Jews said he was making claims to be equal with God and thus that could not be.

> "Therefore the Jews sought the more to kill him, because he not only had broken the Sabbath, but said also that God was his Father, making himself equal with God." (John 5:18) (KJV)

Our early Christian brothers in the face of shear hatred and resistance placed full trust in Jesus' kingdom message. It not only changed their lives, it also impacted the world like was never seen before this time and will never be seen again. They indeed changed an entire civilization through faith. Belief can, it is true, be abstract and totally meaningless but, when God is in the hearts and minds of a people that same powerful energy can be channeled towards all good, combined with the primary fruit of the Spirit, Love, and the gifts that Christ has given the world that of Salvation and Grace, there is perhaps no stronger force which exists on earth. Paul sums it up this way, "If you confess with your mouth, Jesus' is Lord, and believe in your heart that God raised Him from the dead, you will be saved." (Romans 10:9)

Epilogue

Having written all these things down, we find ourselves not at the end of our narrative but merely at a point of summary in short of things that were, things that are and things that are to come. Christian's philosophical views and claims should live out a reality that would outlive them. That same reality of faith-based beliefs has scripted a message that will endure for all time. That enduring message is called the Word and it was birthed by a divine being named Emmanuel, incarnated to be the son of a virgin named Mary and fathered by a man named Joseph. Both of these surrogate parents had lineage bloodline ties to Adam, Shem, Ham and Abraham. The beginning, who was with God before the foundations of the world also known as Christos came robed as flesh that He might be known by men. His purpose was to restore a right-relationship between humanity and God, as man squandered away this gift in the Garden of Eden. The setting for this event occurred on the continent of Africa proper, as did the birth of the child who the prophet Isaiah proclaimed would be called wonderful counselor, Mighty God and Everlasting Father. Historians agree in full that He was born in Africa but now refer to the land as the Middle East. This entire region of Northeastern Africa was land that the Biblical patriarchs dwelled in at one time or another, building their cities, tabernacles, altars etc. The climatic conditions and the geographical location of rivers compassed the Garden point to the sure fact that this fruitful land of God was located somewhere within the land of Saudi Arabia and afar, the ancient land soil of Ethiopia. In Africa, The Messiah was born, crucified and buried and rose from the dead just as the prophet Jonah proclaimed and Isaiah echoed "by His stripes we are healed." We use the prophet Jonah here because we draw a parallel between Jesus and him. Jonah utters his declarative praise from inside the fish and he thanks God for delivering him from drowning in the Mediterranean Sea by rescuing him with the fish. Like Jesus praying that God's will be done before going to the cross, this is seen as an instrument of grace and deliverance, not of some sort of punishment and judgment as if Jesus had done something wrong.[25] But even before all this, as a little child of two or three years of age, the angels commanded his parents whisk him away to the land of Egypt for safe refuge until the evil Herod dies off ensuring his safety. Ah, we know that the angels commanded he be hidden within the midst of the "burnt-face people." We know that upon returning from Egypt he was taken to Nazareth to grow-up and live as a Nazarene studying and reading the scrolls at an early age to discover who he was. We know that the one who God called as, "a messenger to prepare the way before me," baptized Jesus in the river Jordan. In growing up it is important to stress that Jesus grew as a normal child would grow. He was alert to all that was going on around him. He would later use various things he observed as a child to give impartations to the people as words of wisdom. He watched the children as they played in the market place. (Luke 7:32) He noticed the flowers, the trees, the sparrow that fell to the ground, and the foxes in their dens. He heard the shepherd call the sheep by their names. (John 10:3) He learned the lore of the weather. (Matthew 16:2-3) He saw the vine dresser as he pruned the branches of the vine, so that it would bear more fruit. (John15:1-2) All these things he saw and

---

[25] Cracking Old Testament Codes D. Brent Sandy & Ronald L. Giese, Jr.; Broadman and Holman Publishers page 228

remembered and illustrated them in his ministry of teaching. His home was a godly one and this explains where he received the foundations of righteousness. His mother nurtured him keeping the Great Secret, in her heart spurning her to do everything possible for her Firstborn.[26]

The noted author C.S. Lewis, once wrote, "I believe in Christianity as I believe that the sun has risen. Not only because I see it, but because I see everything by it." This body of work has declared itself to be all of the above namely because we "see everything by it," yet we find no ending but only a never-ending story of mankind's struggles with establishing a right-relationship with the Creator of all things under the Heavens and the earth. We've examined the New Testament importance as a direct continuation of the Old Testament times and traditions. We somewhat live our lives to an overarching vision. We compensate where we think we're lacking and overcompensate where we think we have no room at all. Our thoughts are made up of what many of us think without consulting the Word to ascertain what it is that God thinks first. No wonder we cannot guide our lives better than we do. I believe that we

---

[26] [T]he Life and Teachings of Christ Gordon Lindsay Vol 1 His Early Years and Ministry Published by Christ For The Nations, Inc. Dallas, Texas 2005; pages 85 and 86

have our moving and being because God made it so. We are actually all at the last breath of our lives unless God by His Grace and mercies see fit to breath His Nephesh into us in the very next mili-second. Yet for some strange reason we still take God for granted. I wonder what God is going to say too many of us when we stand before the Throne of Grace. Will our works have been enough, or will many of us fall short of His glory. I know that some of the contents within this narrative is such that there will be many who adamantly disagree with my notions and fact-based research. To them I say, when did we stop upholding the Truth? When have we opted out to maintain conjecture and innuendos and falsehoods of an astounding nature? Why have a group of people selected over the course of thousands of years decided to disenfranchise another group of people. Could it be merely for money, power and superiority? I find it hard to believe it's because of hatred for their fellow man. God said one day He "will gather all the people," and bring them back to the land of His promise to Abraham and his seed. I don't know about you the reader but, I don't want to be anywhere around to have to answer for the injustices', disobediences', untruths that have been promulgated against God's children of the first fruits. It would appear to me, "by everything I can see by," a nation of inhabitants have been ostracized and left to make it for themselves without benefit of any of the knowledge and wisdom left for them by their forefathers. It's a solemn occasion when your cultural heritage and His-Story have been stripped away and trashed as if you or your fore parents never existed with their rich cultural values and civilization advances.

In conclusion,

> "Who is he that overcometh the world, but he that believeth that Jesus is the Son of God? This is he that came not by water only, but by water and blood. And it is the Spirit that beareth witness, because the Spirit is truth. For there are three that bear record in Heaven, the Father, the Word, and the Holy Ghost: and these three are one. And there are three that bear witness in earth, the Spirit and the water and the blood: and these three agree in one. If we receive the witness of men, the witness of God is greater: for this is the witness of God which he hath testified of His Son." (I John 5:5-9)

Abraham was the first monotheist in the Bible. As such he believed that there is just one God.[27] We can't pick and choose scripture

---

[27] Webster's New Complete Desk Reference Book Published by Book Essentials Promotions, Windsor Courts New York, 1993

which we're going to believe and substantiate leaving others, which do not fit our rhetoric flow by the wayside. I strongly believe in the written Logos-Holy Bible and to that end all the scripture is "God-breathed," and fundamentally accurate. Abraham was born in the land of Ur or Northeastern Africa. Under God's instructions he journeyed to the land of Canaan. (Modern-day Israel) He was promised the land for himself and his seeds. His seeds followed God's instructions and were obedient. Their seeds David and Solomon all followed suit worshiping the One God. Along comes Jesus within the birthrights and as the prophets of old testified to in the Old Testament. The Messiah is, "One who saves His people." He died, was buried and rose on the third day all on the landscape of Northern Africa. The results of His sacrifice brought about a new era of worship. The movement based upon His name, Christianity or followers, who believed in His teachings and doctrinal message- now called Christians. In His provision of salvation, the believer is a victor. Those who believe and carry forth His message are over comers. Water and blood in the earth is symbolic of Christ as an external objective witness. The Apostle John is battling with those who would teach falsely the dualism in asserting that the Christ-Spirit departed from the man Jesus just prior to His death on the cross. When John writes of the

Spirit of Truth, he no longer emphasizes apostolic testimony but writes of the testimony of God that comes through the Holy Spirit. So because the Spirit of God cannot lie, His testimony is sure. And as sure as that testimony is true so are the facts which uphold the theme of the title and theme of this book; "Bringing the Word from Africa: Cradle of Civilization; Birthplace of Christianity."

AUTOBIOGRAPHICAL

Elder Roger Phillips Sr. is an Ordained Elder serving at Sweet Holy Spirit Church in Chicago, Illinois. He has many organizational and developmental skills with over 20 years of Management Leadership experience. Before retirement, he worked in Sales Management where he was responsible for managing and training salespersons in an automobile sales environment. In addition to sales management he served as Finance Director and Special Markets Finance for high-end imports, pre-driven factory-certified and domestic luxury vehicle lines. Phillips also owned and managed his own transportation limousine company, three franchised muffler and brake shops and Lapels, a men's specialty retail clothing boutique. During this same period, he worked with various community/political organizations as well as consulting marketing work for political for local, county and state government officials.

Elder Phillips has participated in and attended four years of Ministerial praxis training, both onsite field-study and classroom, totaling some 1,800 hours of instruction and ministry field project work. Field study service included; serving as Chief Adjutant and Executive Pastor and 1st assistant to Apostle Jeffrey L. Robinson, Senior Pastor, Eternal Glory 8th Day Apostolic Outreach Ministries. He holds dual Ministerial Licenses and Certificates of Ordination as an Elder of the church from Sweet Holy Spirit Church Apostolic Council and Eternal Glory Apostolic Kingdom Ministries. He is proficient in preaching and expounding the gospel from an Exegetical, Hermeneutical perspective with strong prominence upon substantive scriptural foundations. He instructs in Old and New Testament Theology and Christology in a competent intellectual manner, enhancing the Body of Christ academics and practical understandings. His exceptional skills in elaborating upon hermeneutical issues, allows him to instruct in an advanced manner using correct techniques of text – substance, silence of text interpretations, and sound principle instructions concerning insights and conclusions. He teaches and instructs weekly new members' classes and School of Wisdom classes at Sweet Holy Spirit Church. He was more recently appointed Lead Servant of Sweet Holy Spirit Church Ministerial Alliance, the organized body of Elders, Ministers, Ministers-in-Training and Aspirants. In the capacity of one of the Assistant Pastors, he trains and instructs the ecclesia on ministerial ethics and methods of operating within the walls of the church as well as outside, releasing their individual gifts for the betterment and advancement of the Body of Christ. With his firm grasp of Biblical/Theological knowledge and church historical issues, he has written a sound academic instruction curriculum for the Adult Christian Education programs as directed by the Episcopal Office of Bishop Larry D. Trotter and the Church Council of Apostolic Presbyters. He also authors and instructs academic training programs for Licensed Ministers, Ministers-in-training and Aspirants within the Alliance under authority of the Apostolic Council and Episcopal office. In December of 2012, Phillips was elevated to the office of Overseer-Vicar to the Presiding Prelate of New Century Fellowship of Churches and Ministries International. Elder Phillips graduated from Newburgh College of the Bible with a B.A. degree in Biblical Studies and Newburgh Theological Seminary with an M.A. degree in advanced Biblical studies. He completed his Doctor of Philosophy studies at Newburgh Theological Seminary and was conferred a PhD degree in Biblical and Theological Studies at Newburgh, Indiana. He has currently enrolled in a special Doctor of Philosophy program of study in Sacred Divinity and will graduate with his second PhD in 2016.

MAPS

Before the opening of the Suez Canal (1869) which is essentially a man-made body of water which extends from the Red Sea to the Mediterranean, the region of the world now known as the Middle East was actually considered a part of Africa. It was quite simply the Northeastern most corner of the continent of Africa. There were no geographic, geological, cultural, racial or empirical barriers which separated the two lands. There were absolutely no foreign trade routes, environmental terrain or unfamiliar civilizations existing without the express knowledge of the entire whole of Africa. The inhabitants of the so-called Middle East were one and the same.

To be more laconic in this statement of fact, the original inhabitants of the land were Africans. The various philosophies and opinions as well as innovations developed in this land, are undoubtedly all African, emendating from African minds in an African environment. Linguistically, genetically, culturally, yes indeed, pure African. The usage of the deceptive Euro-centric term 'middle east' was seemly another clever ruse to doctrinally invoke and lay claim to the landscape of Northeastern Africa.

1

God said, *"out of Egypt, have I called my son" (Matthew 2:15)* Indeed He did, for some of the world's most profound, historically powerful and spiritually significant people places and ideology arose from out of this land. The excising of this vast land literally cut Israel, Mecca, and the Sinai Peninsula off among others from mother Africa. Mesopotamia is considered the cradle of civilization; however, because of this newly designed construct called the Middle East, or Near East, or Asia Minor, most of the world has been led to believe a lie and disassociate itself with any African presence.

The various maps and illustrations herein are only for the reader to grasp a factual knowledge of the land mass before the separation and confirm the continent of Africa was all inclusive of the now named Middle East. Hopefully the reader will gain some historical realities concerning the truth about the people of the Bible and their identities.

Why didn't Joseph's brothers recognize him when they journeyed to Egypt to buy food during the famine? If he was any other complexion unlike the Egyptians, he would have stood out amongst them. How could Moses be raised as an Egyptian in the house of Pharaoh (40 years) if he were any other complexion other than black skinned and not be detected? If Moses wasn't black skinned, why would the daughters of Midian (located in Saudi Arabia) refer to him as, "an Egyptian delivered us out of the hand of the shepherds...." (Exodus 2:19) Lastly, "And He said, put thine hand into thy bosom *again. And he put his hand into his bosom again; and plucked it out of his bosom, and, behold, it turned again as his other flesh."* *(Exodus 4:7)* When Moses first placed his hand in his bosom, *"it was leprous as **snow."*** What color I submit, is snow? Moses, Joseph and his brothers were all Hebrews, dwelling in the land of Africa, Birthplace of Christianity.

ILLUSTRATIONS

PANGAEA MAPS

Map No. 1

PERMIAN
225 million years ago

TRIASSIC
200 million years ago

JURASSIC
135 million years ago

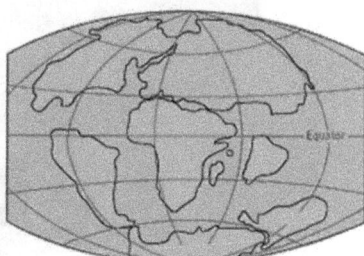

CRETACEOUS
65 million years ago

PRESENT DAY

Map No. 2

God created man and placed him in the Garden of Eden, in west Asia, … indicated by the black square [on the map].

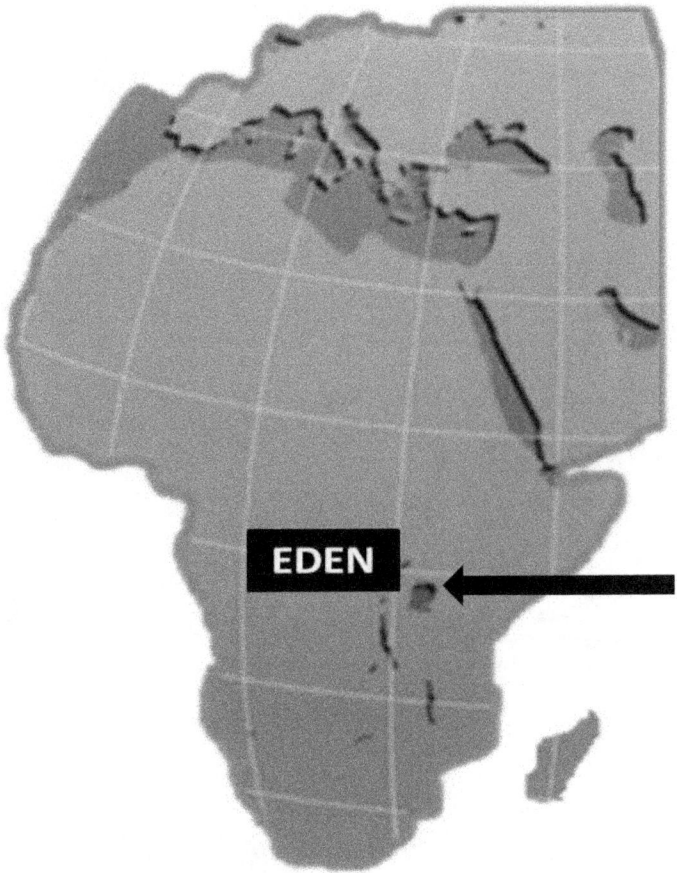

Map No. 3

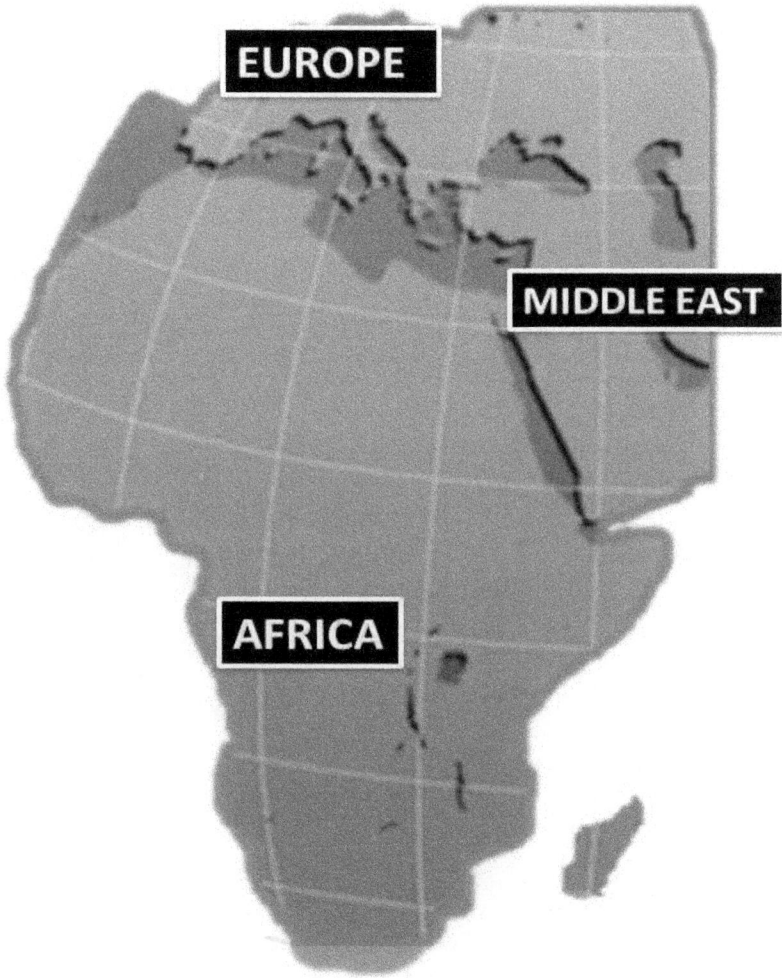

Map No. 4

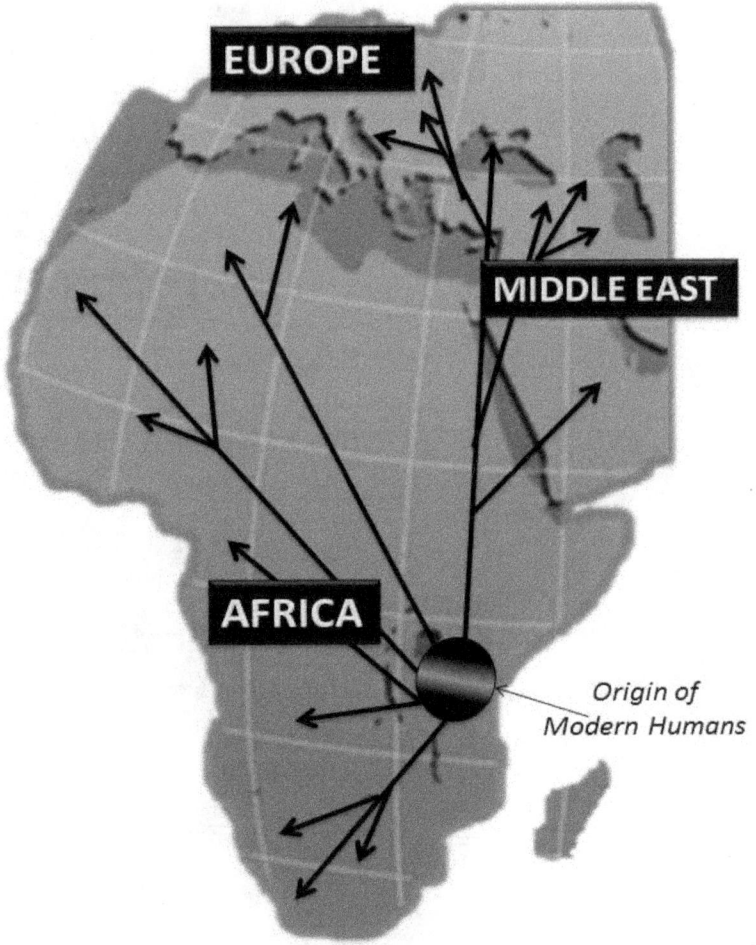

EUROPE

MIDDLE EAST

AFRICA

*Origin of
Modern Humans*

Map No. 5

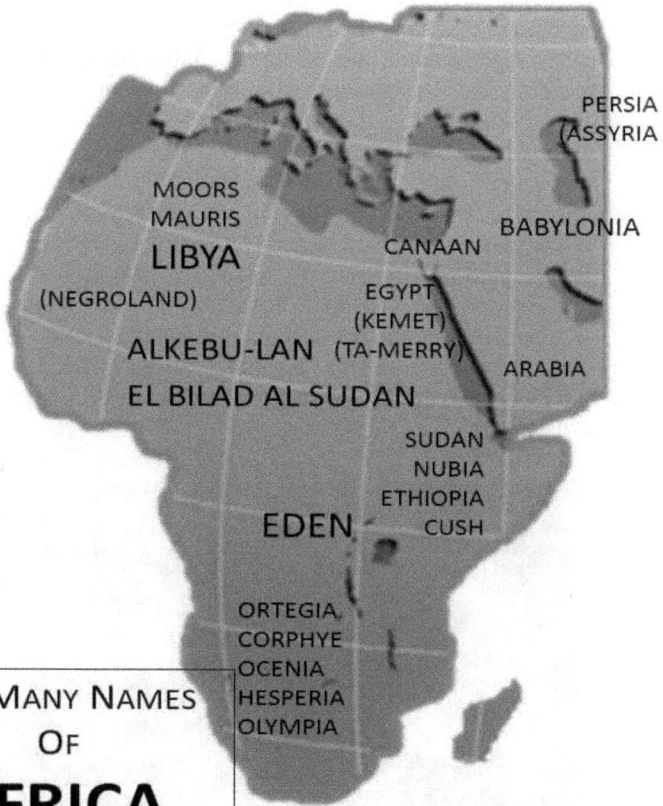

PERSIA
(ASSYRIA

MOORS
MAURIS
BABYLONIA
CANAAN
LIBYA
(NEGROLAND)
EGYPT
(KEMET)
ALKEBU-LAN (TA-MERRY)
ARABIA
EL BILAD AL SUDAN

SUDAN
NUBIA
ETHIOPIA
EDEN CUSH

ORTEGIA
CORPHYE
OCENIA
THE MANY NAMES HESPERIA
OF OLYMPIA

AFRICA
(THE LAND OF HAM)

Map No. 6

The Khazars, a people of Turkic origin, converted to the Jewish religion sometime in the 9th century, beginning with the royal house and spreading gradually among the general populace. Judaism is now known to have been more widespread among the Khazar inhabitants of the Khazar kingdom than was previously thought. Eastern European Jews were assuredly of the Khazar bloodline, rather than the Abrahamic bloodline. In 1999, Russian archaeologists announced that they had successfully reconstructed a Khazarian vessel from the Don River region, revealing 4 inscriptions of the word "Israel" in Hebrew lettering. It is now the accepted opinion among most scholars in the field that the conversion of the Khazars to Judaism was widespread, and not limited merely to the royal house and nobility. Ibn al-Faqih, in fact, wrote "All of the Khazars are Jews." Christian of Stavelot wrote in 864 that "all of them profess the Jewish faith in its entirety."

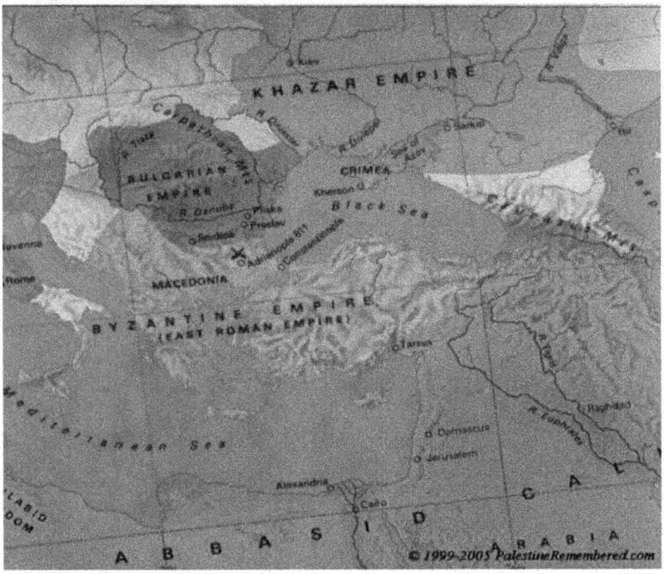

BIBLIOGRAPHY

Lockyer, Sr., Herbert General Editor: Nelson's Illustrated Bible Dictionary. Nashville, Tennessee: Thomas Nelson Publishers 1986

Wegener, Alfred Dr., Translated by John Biram. The Origin of Continents and Oceans. Dover Publications, Inc. 1966. 4th revised edition Die Entstehung der Kontinente und Ozeane. Friedr. Vieweg 7 Sohn, Braunschweig 1929

Halley, H. Henry. Halleys Bible Handbook. Grand Rapids, Michigan: Zondervan Publishing House 23rd edition 1962

Felder P.h.D, Rev Cain Hope. General Editor: The Original African Heritage Study Bible KJV 2nd Printing, Nashville, Tennessee: The James C. Winston Publishing Company 1993

Strong, James LL.D., S.T.D.: The New Strong's Exhaustive Concordance of the Bible: Nashville, Tennessee: Thomas Nelson Publishers 1990

(http://www.truthknowledge.com/gfacts_about_mil e: The Internet Answer Engine

Vogel O. Joseph: Encyclopedia of Pre-Colonial Africa: Walnut Creek, California: Sage Publications, Inc. Altamira Press 1997

Murray, Jocelyn. Cultural Atlas of Africa: New York, N.Y. Checkmark Books 1981

Evans, McKee William. From The Land of Canaan to the Land of Guinea: The Strange Odyssey of the Sons of Ham. The American Historical Review Volume 85(pp 17-18) No 1 1981 Chicago, IL University of Chicago Press

Landau I., Sidney Editor in Chief: Funk & Wagnalls Standard Desk Dictionary. New York, N.Y. Funk & Wagnalls Publishing Co., Inc. 1969

(http://en.wikipedia.org/wiki/Israel Demographics of Israel)

Bridger, David, Wolk, Samuel. The New Jewish Encyclopedia. Springfield, New Jersey Behrman House Publishing. 1976

Wigoder, Geoffrey. The New Standard Jewish Encyclopedia. Garden City, New York Double Day and Company 1992

Weiland, Ted R. God's Covenant People: Yesterday, today, and forever. Grand Rapids, Michigan, William B. Eerdmans Publishing Company 1992

Bernstein, Jack. The Life of an American Jew in Racist Marxist Isreal. Newport Beach, California 1984

Gaebelein, Frank E. The Expositor's Bible Community Volume I NIV. Grand Rapids, Michigan. Zondervan 1979

www.ingramcontent.com/pod-product-compliance
Lightning Source LLC
Chambersburg PA
CBHW051845090426
42811CB00034B/2220/J